The

Myth

of Judicial

Activism

THE
MYTH
OF JUDICIAL
ACTIVISM

Making Sense of
Supreme Court Decisions

KERMIT ROOSEVELT III

Yale University Press   New Haven and London

Set in Minion type by Integrated Publishing Solutions.
Printed in the United States of America.

The Library of Congress has cataloged the hardcover edition as follows:
Roosevelt, Kermit, 1971–
The myth of judicial activism : making sense of Supreme Court
decisions / Kermit Roosevelt III.
    p. cm.
Includes bibliographical references and index.
ISBN-13: 978-0-300-11468-3 (hardcover : alk. paper)
ISBN-10: 0-300-11468-0 (hardcover : alk. paper)
1. United States. Supreme Court.   2. Political questions and judicial
power—United States.   I. Title.
KF8742.R65 2006
347.73'26—dc22   2006013002

ISBN 978-0-300-12691-4 (pbk. : alk. paper)

A catalogue record for this book is available from the British Library.

The paper in this book meets the guidelines for permanence and
durability of the Committee on Production Guidelines for Book
Longevity of the Council on Library Resources.

10 9 8 7 6 5 4 3 2 1

To America's judges

Contents

Acknowledgments

This book would not exist without the interest and inspiration of Akhil Amar and Michael O'Malley. In writing it, I have been greatly aided by the advice and comments of friends, family, students, and colleagues—categories that in some cases overlap. For their help, I am grateful to my parents, my sister Corinne, Jack Balkin, Justin C. Danilewitz, David Franklin, Larry Hardesty, Melissa Iachan, Ted Ruger, Stephen F. Williams, and Jie Yuan. None should be held responsible for the results. Felicia Lewis deserves special thanks for her encouragement and patience.

Introduction:
Judging the Court

After eleven years without a vacancy on the Supreme Court, the year 2005 brought two. The president nominated D.C. Circuit Court judge John Roberts to succeed William Rehnquist as Chief Justice, and the Senate readily confirmed him. White House counsel Harriet Miers, the president's choice to replace Sandra Day O'Connor, encountered more resistance. Concerned about her lack of relevant legal experience, and uncertain of Miers's views on constitutional issues, even conservatives offered lukewarm support or outright opposition. Twenty-four days after announcing the nomination, President Bush withdrew it. His next pick was Samuel Alito, a judge on the federal court of appeals for the Third Circuit. Though the Alito hearings were somewhat more contentious than those of John Roberts, the Senate eventually confirmed him by a vote of 58 to 42.

The process of nomination and confirmation gives the American people, through their elected representatives, the chance to say what they want in terms of constitutional interpretation. On that question, the answer seemed clear. President Bush had promised that his nominees would "exercise not the will of men, but the judgment of law."[1] In his introductions of the Roberts and Alito nominations, he returned to the theme. Roberts, President Bush announced, would "strictly apply the Constitution and laws, not legislate from the bench."[2] Alito, Bush said, "understands that judges are to interpret the laws, not to impose their preferences or priorities on the people."[3]

The senators who interviewed Roberts before confirming him made the same point. Senator Jeff Sessions complained about "[a]ctivist rulings not based on statutes or the Constitution," and Senator Tom Coburn lamented that "[d]ecades of judicial activism have created these huge rifts in the social fabric of our country." Senator Richard Durbin expressed concern about overuse of the activist label, noting that it had been applied to a Republican-appointed Alabama judge for decisions protecting civil rights marchers. But everyone seemed to agree that activism was bad.

So the Supreme Court confirmation hearings taught us that the American people want judges who will faithfully apply the law, who will not allow their personal preferences to influence their professional work. But that is to say that they taught us essentially nothing at all—that "lesson" is at once crashingly obvious and more or less empty of content. As Senator Coburn admitted, "[w]e each have our own definition of judicial activism." To agree that activism is bad means nothing if we cannot also agree on what counts as activism.

The Supreme Court confirmation hearings, sadly, did not help us with this second issue. No one explained how to identify activism in any objective way, and the nominees resolutely refused to offer anything more than vague platitudes about their respective approaches to constitutional interpretation. Certainly they would not be lured into a discussion of whether specific decisions could be justified.

This book seeks to shed light on the question of what justifies a constitutional decision. It does not do so by developing a theory of activism, for in practice "activist" turns out to be little more than a rhetorically charged shorthand for decisions the speaker disagrees with. In place of the overworked concept of activism, this book offers the idea of legitimacy. To say that a decision is legitimate, as I will use the term, basically means that the Supreme Court has taken a reasonable position in terms of deferring or not deferring to the government body whose action it is reviewing—the president or Congress, if the case involves the federal government, or state legislatures or executives if the case involves states. (How to decide whether that position is reasonable is the topic of chapter 2.) It does not mean that the decision is compelled by the Constitution, or that it is the only legitimate resolution of the problem before the Court. But it means that the chosen resolution is within the realm of acceptable judicial behavior, and the Court cannot be condemned for it. I hope that the concept of legitimacy will allow for more productive discussions of the Court's work.

One goal of this book is thus to allow us to assess the new Court's performance as we go forward. Another is more focused on the present and the past. Recent years have seen a surprising level of hostility toward the Supreme Court and toward judges more generally, and I will suggest that this hostility is unwarranted. To that end, I analyze Supreme Court decisions, showing how the standard of legitimacy I have developed applies to a wide range of cases—some of which most everyone agrees are right; some that are deeply divisive; and some that most everyone agrees were mistakes. I try to show that once we move beyond the misleadingly simplistic rhetoric of activism, most Supreme Court decisions are in fact legitimate. When the Supreme Court goes badly astray, the mistake generally comes because it has refused to defer to some other governmental actor that is better placed to decide the relevant question, or conversely because it has blindly deferred to an actor it ought not to have trusted. That is, asking whether the Court has employed the appropriate level of deference will do a pretty good job of picking out the truly bad decisions.

I do not expect that all readers will agree with my conclusions, but I hope that the approach I set out will allow us to identify the grounds of our disagreement and discuss them more constructively. Whether the Court is deferring or not is a question that can be answered objectively. Whether deference is appropriate is a harder question, and it does not have an objectively correct answer. But the set of factors that supports deference or a refusal to defer is a limited one, and if we are arguing over their relative significance, I believe we are talking about the right thing.

I try to explain and apply my standard of legitimacy in a relatively straightforward and accessible fashion. This book is not written exclusively, or even primarily, for lawyers. I hope that it has some insights that lawyers and law students will find interesting, but my primary goal has been to write something that will be illuminating and useful to non-lawyers. Supreme Court opinions are highly complicated and technical. Assessing the intricacies of the decisions is difficult, if not impossible, for anyone other than a specialist in that particular area of law. What I have tried to offer here is a method of evaluation that does not require any specialized knowledge, or any familiarity with long and tangled strings of precedent. It relies on simple and commonsense understandings of what the Constitution means, and equally commonsense considerations about whether judges or other governmental actors are better at determining whether a given act complies with that meaning. What I have tried to do, in other words, is to offer a perspective from which citizens can judge the Court.

The book contains five parts. Part one is the theoretical part. It offers a description of constitutional decision-making that distinguishes between the meaning of the Constitution and the rules that judges create to implement that meaning, what I will call constitutional doctrine. It explains the factors that go into the creation of doctrine, and it uses them to develop a standard by which the legitimacy of doctrine can be assessed. This standard suggests that the key disagreement among Supreme Court justices, frequently, is not about constitutional meaning but rather about how much deference the Court should give to the judgment of other government actors. The key question for legitimacy, likewise, will frequently be what explanation can be given for the Court's decision to defer or not to defer.

Parts two, three, and four form the body of the book. They take the model developed in the first part and apply it to actual Supreme Court cases, attempting to explain why and how these decisions can or cannot be called legitimate. In these parts, I discuss most of the Court's recent controversial decisions, dealing with topics including abortion, the death penalty, affirmative action, gay rights, the war on terror, and the taking of private property for public use. I also discuss some older cases, in order to see what we can learn from decisions that are now either universally accepted or universally rejected. Part Five considers what the survey of cases can teach us about activism and legitimacy, and about the question of whether the Supreme Court has become too powerful, as its critics charge.

The theoretical part of the book is essential to set up the discussion that follows. The discussions of the individual cases are freestanding, and readers who are not interested in particular topics should feel free to skip them. At the end of each chapter I have included a section entitled "Further Reading." These sections will suggest other works that expand on, or deny, some of the arguments I make. Although law review articles are the standard form of legal scholarship, I have tried where possible to identify books that are more easily available to the general public.

These sections will also identify issues I did not feel able to address adequately in the main text and point readers to useful discussions of those topics. As I do no more than note the issues, some parts of those sections may seem cryptic. Constitutional law is simple in some ways, and I hope that the analysis of the main text is readily accessible. It can become quite complicated in other ways—chiefly once we start to think about academic analysis and Supreme Court doctrine as well as the Constitution itself—and in the "Further Reading" sections I cannot do full justice to those complexities. I hope that the sections will answer some of the questions that may occur to lawyers or academics who read the book, but they can also be skimmed or skipped without compromising my main objective.

That objective—helping citizens to understand and evaluate the work of the Supreme Court—is crucial to the health of our constitutional democracy. Supreme Court decisions are tremendously important. They deal with hot-button social issues like abortion, affirmative action, and gay rights, and also with deep and abstract questions about the structure of our government, like the scope of federal legislative power and the authority of the president during wartime. These are issues with which every citizen should be concerned.

Sadly, the Court frequently writes opinions that are accessible only to specialists. It is that inaccessibility that allows partisans to paint the decisions as nothing more than reflections of the justices' political preferences. But the Constitution does not belong to judges, as a mystery intelligible only to a priestly caste, and it does not belong to political activists, as a set of incendiary talking points. It belongs to the people. It is our responsibility to judge the Court, and it is our judgment that must be decisive in the end.

I
Deciding
Constitutional Cases

1

The Plain Meaning of the Constitution: The Fallacy of Direct Enforcement

On April 8, 2005, critics of the Supreme Court gathered in Washington at a conference entitled "Remedies to Judicial Tyranny." Several speakers suggested that impeachment would be an appropriate response to some of the Court's recent decisions. One, Edwin Vieira, endorsed removal by quoting Stalin's slogan "No man, no problem." (Stalin, if not Vieira, had something other than impeachment in mind: the full quotation is "Death solves everything: no man, no problem.")[1]

On April 24, 2005, and again on August 14, religious leaders held an event they called "Justice Sunday," intended to educate "values voters" about the threats posed by judges. In May 2005, televangelist Pat Robertson pronounced that judges "destroying the fabric that holds the nation together" are a menace "probably more serious than a few bearded terrorists who fly into buildings."[2] The comparison is surprising, but in March 2005 the Pentagon released a document placing judges in the same company. Titled "The National Defense Strategy of the United States of America," the document warned that "our strength as a nation state will continue to be challenged by those who employ a strategy of the weak using international fora, judicial processes, and terrorism."[3]

What has provoked this sense of outrage against the judiciary? What is it that judges are doing wrong? And what should they be doing instead? The criticism is made with different degrees of sophistication, but at bottom the critics say the same thing. Activist judges, they claim, are substituting their own political preferences for the mandates of the Constitution. They are exercising will, not judgment; they are imposing their own values on society. In his statement announcing support for a Federal Marriage Amendment, President Bush warned that "the sacred institution of marriage should not be redefined by a few activist judges." Within the Supreme Court itself, Justice Antonin Scalia has criticized his colleagues for abandoning "text and tradition" in favor of "philosophical predilection and moral intuition."[4] Perhaps most notable, a book-length denunciation of the Supreme Court's supposed activism recently spent a considerable number of weeks on the *New York Times* best-seller list.

That book is Mark Levin's *Men in Black: How the Supreme Court Is Destroying America.*[5] I will refer to it frequently in the pages that follow, not because it is the best statement of the charge of activism, but because it seems to be the most widely read, and, as we shall see, it illustrates some of the weaknesses of the argument. Levin's assertions blend easily into the growing chorus. Activist judges, he writes, "have abused their constitutional mandate by imposing their personal prejudices and beliefs on the rest of society."[6] They "make, rather than in-terpret, the law."[7]

The charge of activism makes for good rhetoric. The im-position of judges' values on the rest of us amounts to rule by an unelected elite in defiance of the most basic principles of American democracy. The sound bites are easy to manufacture and hard to rebut. No one, after all, would argue that judicial activism is a good thing.

Precisely because the specter of government by judiciary strikes such a deep chord with Americans, its threat has been a near-constant refrain. The danger was raised by Abraham Lin-coln, who warned that if policy questions were placed in the hands of judges, "the people will have ceased to be their own rulers."[8] It was raised by Theodore Roosevelt, who denied "that the American people have surrendered to any set of men, no matter what their position or their character, the final right to determine those fundamental questions upon which free self-government ultimately depends."[9] And it was raised by Theo-dore's cousin Franklin, who accused the Supreme Court of "acting not as a judicial body, but as a policy-making body" in striking down New Deal legislation. FDR offered a concrete solution—a plan to add new justices to the Court—and char-acterized his proposal as "action to save the Constitution from the Court."[10]

Lincoln and the Roosevelts are generally considered good presidents, and the Supreme Court decisions they opposed have not fared well in the judgment of history. But the rheto-ric of judicial activism has been deployed by those who ended up on the losing side of history as well. Sixty years ago, the enforcement of Bill of Rights liberties such as the freedom of speech against the states (rather than merely the federal gov-ernment) was denounced as activism, but the proposition that the First Amendment binds the states is now embedded in our legal culture and generally considered correct. Much the same can be said of many of the Supreme Court decisions of the 1960s that broadened the constitutional protections for criminal defendants: they were intensely controversial at the time, and some critics remain, but on the whole those decisions are now considered both legitimate and unassailable.

The most striking example of a successful "activist" decision is probably *Brown v. Board of Education*, which held public school segregation unconstitutional. Almost no one nowadays disputes that *Brown* was correctly decided—indeed, Mark Levin argues that *Plessy v. Ferguson*, which endorsed the idea of "separate but equal," and which *Brown* overruled, was the activist decision.[11] But in 1953, when it was decided, many leading legal scholars thought that *Brown* was pure activism: a morally and politically appealing result, perhaps, but not one that could be justified by reference to the Constitution. *Brown*'s opponents took a still dimmer view; the segregationists' 1956 Southern Manifesto denounced the decision as "a clear abuse of judicial power."[12]

What does this survey show? The Supreme Court has been called activist by good politicians and bad ones, by those whose judgment history would vindicate, and by those whose views are now marginal and discredited. It has been called activist by pro-Union Republicans in the 1860s, by Progressives in the 1920s, by New Deal Democrats in the 1930s, by segregationists in the 1950s, by conservatives in the 1970s and 1980s. And though the complaints about judicial activism are heard most frequently from conservatives in the early twenty-first century, liberals are rediscovering the phrase as well. Recent books on the subject argue that the Rehnquist Court displayed "activism on the right" and was in fact "the most activist Supreme Court in history."[13]

In short, the Supreme Court has been castigated for activism almost continuously, from quite early on and by a wide variety of critics. If the charge of activism is to be anything more than a political talking point—and it should surprise no one that, frequently, that is all it is—we need some way of determining when the charge is justified and when it is not. We need some way of deciding whether a given decision is activist.

Most critics start out by saying that the decisions they call activist are wrong. But activism is more than error, and the next step is thus to argue that the error is so blatant that it cannot be a good faith mistake; it must be the deliberate imposition of the judge's own preferences in defiance of the Constitution. The plausibility of the charge of activism thus depends at least implicitly on the idea that there is a clearly correct answer (frequently called "the plain meaning of the Constitution") that judges are disregarding. And the basic reason that the term "activism" has no place in a serious discussion is that relatively few significant or controversial cases possess clear right answers.

That is not to say that there are never obvious answers to constitutional questions. The Constitution does contain some very clear rules. It provides that a bill will become a law if it is passed by both houses of Congress and signed by the president. It sets minimum age requirements for holding elected office: twenty-five years for representatives, thirty for senators, and thirty-five for president. But these are not the constitutional provisions about which disagreement exists. Controversial decisions deal with the meaning of provisions such as the First Amendment's protection of speech and religious exercise, or the Fourteenth Amendment's guarantees of due process and equal protection.

The complaint that judges are departing from the plain meaning of the Constitution has very little force with respect to these sorts of provisions, for the words of the Constitution themselves convey very little information about how to decide particular cases. The guarantee of equal protection, for instance, surely means that the government cannot refuse some people the shelter of its laws—something the Reconstruction Congress was quite concerned about, given the failure of southern states to protect newly freed slaves from violence at the hands of nightriders and Klansmen. It has also consistently been interpreted to prevent certain kinds of government discrimination. But which kinds?

Almost all laws could be characterized as discriminatory. Even an ordinary criminal law—for instance, the law against burglary—discriminates between those who commit burglary and those who do not. And even if we exclude "discrimination" based solely on conduct, discriminatory governmental practices are legion. The tax code grants preferential treatment to homeowners and married couples. State universities discriminate among applicants based on test scores, grade point averages, geographical origin, alumni parents, and nebulous "diversity" considerations. States employ similar considerations when hiring employees. Even age or vision requirements for driver's licenses discriminate. Some of these practices may be constitutionally problematic, and some are surely acceptable. But the words of the Constitution do not tell us which is which.

The First Amendment's prohibition on laws "abridging the freedom of speech" is no more self-explanatory than equal protection. Does a law whose incidental effect is to make speech harder to engage in constitute a forbidden abridgement? What about a governmental choice to fund some speakers but not others, or to make funds generally available to private speakers as long as they do not express a particular disfavored viewpoint? What if the government itself imposes no penalties on speakers but allows other private individuals to sue them for damages? Is flag-burning speech? Is a donation to a political campaign? These are all important questions, but none of them is answered by the words of the First Amendment alone.

Men in Black offers several neat, if inadvertent, examples of the difficulties one encounters in trying to maintain that the plain meaning of the Constitution resolves controversial cases. With respect to the Equal Protection Clause, Levin takes the Supreme Court to task for holding that if married couples are allowed access to contraception, single people must be given the same right. "Nowhere," Levin writes, "does the Constitution require that married couples and single people be treated the same where contraception is involved."[14] That is quite true as far as the words themselves are concerned—the Equal Protection Clause does not say anything about marriage or contraception. But neither does it say anything about race (unlike the adjacent Fifteenth Amendment, which specifically forbids states from denying the right to vote "on account of race"). The absence of any mention of race makes it hard to argue on the basis of the Constitution's words alone, as Levin later does, that "[t]he Fourteenth Amendment prohibits all state discrimination based on race, without exception."[15]

With respect to the First Amendment, Levin claims that "[t]he framers could not have been clearer about what they meant or about their intentions"[16] and goes on to denounce the Supreme Court for allowing some restrictions on campaign contributions. But whatever we may say about whether giving money to politicians should be protected activity, it is not speech in any obvious, literal sense—and it is farther removed from literal speech than expressive conduct such as burning a flag in protest.

Eventually, the argument that Levin's preferred results are commanded by the "plain meaning" of the Constitution reaches a peak of absurdity as he protests that the Court "went so far as to extend the term 'person' in the Fourteenth Amendment to include illegal aliens."[17] Again, there may be strong arguments that an illegal alien should not be entitled to claim rights under the Fourteenth Amendment. But that such a person is not a "person" according to the plain meaning of the word is not one of them.

So a judge cannot simply enforce the plain meaning of the Constitution. This is not because the meaning is not clear. It is because the clear meaning exists at a relatively high level of generality. The Equal Protection Clause forbids unjustified discrimination; most Supreme Court justices would agree on that. But agreement that unjustified discrimination violates the Constitution is not agreement on much. It is not agreement about how specific cases should come out, for as Justice Oliver Wendell Holmes famously put it, general propositions do not decide concrete cases.[18] It remains to be decided which acts of discrimination are justified and which are not. How to do that is a complicated issue, one which I will address at greater length in chapter 3. (In particular, I will consider the argument that supplementing text with history allows us to determine what the Constitution means for specific cases.) The point here is simply that the plain meaning does not get us all the way to a decision. The idealized opposite of judicial activism—what I call "direct enforcement" of the Constitution—

turns out to be a fantasy. And if direct enforcement is illusory, identifying activism may be harder than we supposed.

To decide what judicial behavior is legitimate, we have to understand what judges actually do in deciding constitutional cases. That requires moving beyond the false dichotomy between activism and enforcement. But if judges do not engage in direct enforcement, what do they do? What I have suggested above is that judges can seldom take the plain words of the Constitution and use them to decide particular cases. Something is needed to mediate between the words of the Constitution and specific judicial decisions. Constitutional decision-making is going to be more complicated than simply applying some plain meaning.

Indeed it is. It is very complicated. Read some Supreme Court opinions and you will learn that, if little else. You will encounter tiers of scrutiny, five-factor tests, requirements of congruence and proportionality, and undue burden analysis. You will find a host of bewildering distinctions, between content-based and content-neutral regulations of speech, between hard and soft money, between intentional discrimination and disparate impact. All these and more await new law students and citizens bold enough to venture into the work product of their nation's highest court.

It will be very easy to see that Supreme Court decisions never just apply the words of the Constitution. Indeed, they focus very little on the words. What they focus on instead—what all the obscurities I have just mentioned are—is doctrine. Doctrine is the nitty-gritty of constitutional adjudication. It is the set of rules that the Supreme Court creates to take it from the grand language of the Constitution to the actual outcomes of particular cases. In deciding cases, the Court does not ask whether the governmental act it reviews is consistent with the meaning of the Constitution; it asks whether the act is consistent with the Court's doctrine.

The mere existence of doctrine poses a problem for the proponents of direct enforcement. None of these tests and distinctions is there in the Constitution itself. If legitimate judicial behavior is limited to enforcing the plain meaning of the Constitution, then no modern Supreme Court decision is legitimate.

But no one condemns the Court to that extent. At least some doctrine is legitimate, even if the rules it imposes are not found in the Constitution. The question—the basic question this book seeks to answer—is what makes doctrine legitimate. How can we distinguish between rules that are justifiable as ways to implement constitutional meaning and those that distort the Constitution?

To answer this question, we first need to establish the purpose of doctrine. Because direct enforcement of "plain meaning" is impossible, the next natural thought might be that doctrine is designed to lead the Court to decide cases correctly according to the meaning of the Constitution—to uphold governmental acts that are consistent with the Constitution and to strike down those that are not, even if discovering that meaning takes some work. Doctrine is complicated, on this account, because constitutional meaning is hard to figure out, but its purpose is relatively simple. The straightforward goal of producing correct decisions suggests an equally simple standard of legitimacy: doctrine is legitimate, one might think, to the extent that it leads to correct decisions. The Court's aspiration, according to this theory, is to reach the right answer in all cases, to enforce the Constitution perfectly.

This certainly sounds plausible, but I will argue that it is another misconception. As the next chapter discusses, the Supreme Court is but one actor in a complicated political system. The factors it must take into account in creating doctrine go well beyond the simple desire to maximize the accuracy of its decisions. In a number of circumstances, doctrine is deliberately crafted with the knowledge that it will lead the Court to uphold some governmental acts that violate the meaning of the Constitution, or to strike down some that do not. That is, some doctrinal rules will lead the Court to get cases *wrong* according to the meaning of the Constitution. Perfect enforcement is just as much a fallacy as direct enforcement. The next chapter explains why, and it develops an account of the factors that actually guide the Supreme Court in its creation of doctrine.

Further Reading

For recent criticism of the Court, from the right and the left, one may consult, in addition to *Men in Black,* Martin Garbus, *Courting Disaster: The Supreme Court and the Unmaking of American Law* (Times Books, 2003); Thomas M. Keck, *The Most Activist Supreme Court in History: The Road to Modern Judicial Conservatism* (University of Chicago Press, 2004); Pat Robertson, *Courting Disaster: How the Supreme Court Is Usurping the Power of Congress and the People* (Integrity Publishers, 2004); Herman Schwartz, ed., *The Rehnquist Court: Judicial Activism on the Right* (Hill and Wang, 2002); Christopher Wolfe, ed., *That Eminent Tribunal: Judicial Supremacy and the Constitution* (Princeton University Press, 2004).

2

The Model:
What Doctrine Is For

One of the things that the Supreme Court does is decide individual cases. Its obligation in those cases is to provide justice to the litigants before it, and the most important aspect of that obligation is probably to get the right answer to the question the case presents. But the Supreme Court has other roles. It is not just a court deciding cases; it is also the head of one of the three branches of the federal government, and the doctrine that it creates is designed to do a good deal more (and in some circumstances less) than simply get the right answer. The best way to see this is to walk through the reasoning process that the Supreme Court might actually follow in the creation of the doctrinal rules it uses to decide cases.

Consider a hypothetical Court that starts with the modest aim of getting the right answer as frequently as possible. At first blush, this objective might suggest keeping doctrine very simple. The doctrinal rule adopted to implement a particular constitutional provision should stay as close as possible to the meaning of that provision. Suppose the Court is dealing with the Equal Protection Clause, which says that no state may "deny to any person within its jurisdiction the equal protection of the laws." And suppose it has decided that the meaning of this provision is essentially that the government may not treat some people worse than others without sufficient justification. More precisely, the demand for an adequate justification can be understood to contain two components. First, the government may never treat some people worse than others out of a desire to harm those people, and second, even if it does not act out of hostility, it cannot discriminate unless the benefits of its classification outweigh the burdens: unless the discrimination is in the public interest because it offers net benefits to society.

The doctrinal rule the Court would follow, then, might simply restate this interpretation of the Equal Protection Clause. If the discrimination is not the product of hostility and confers benefits that outweigh the burdens it imposes, the government will win. If not, the individual who has been discriminated against will win. (In order to decide an actual case, the Court would also have to determine whether the individual or the government bears the burden of persuasion, but we will leave that aside for the moment.)

However, matters are not quite that simple. When the constitutionality of government action is challenged, the government (either state or federal) appears as one of the litigants. Article VI of the Constitution requires every government official, both state and federal, to take an oath to support the Constitution. (It is one of the striking features of American government that the primary object of loyalty is not a person, a party, an office, or even a nation, but the Constitution itself.) Thus, governmental action carries with it at least the implicit judgment of the governmental actor that what has been done is in compliance with the Constitution. In the equal protection case, this would be an implicit judgment that whatever burdens are inflicted on the group that is being discriminated against are not the product of hostility and are outweighed by the benefits of discrimination. The Court is in part reviewing the governmental action, but it is also in part reviewing the judgment of the governmental actor.

If the Court is concerned simply with getting the right answer as often as possible, why should it care what other governmental actors think? Because the Court can make mistakes. It cannot be reversed, because no higher court exists, but it can still get things wrong. (Justice Robert Jackson once joked that the Court is not final because it is infallible, but rather it is infallible because it is final.)[1] On some questions, other institutions might be better at determining the right answer. The relative abilities of the Court and the other actor to determine the right answer is the first factor the Court must take into account. I call it "institutional competence."

Institutional Competence

With respect to the question of whether a particular discriminatory law is motivated by hostility, the legislature that enacts that law is obviously in a better position to know than the Court. If the legislature is acting in good faith—an important "if"— then the possibility of obtaining right answers to that question will be increased if the Court does not attempt to decide the matter itself but simply accepts the legislative judgment.

The same is probably generally true of the second component of the equal protection requirement, that the discrimination confer net benefits. The costs and benefits of a law are difficult to calculate. They may depend on complex factual analysis, and they may depend on the intensity of preferences among the people affected. Legislatures can conduct hearings on the effects of laws; they can receive testimony from affected people and from experts. Courts can do similar things, but they do so within the narrow context of an adversarial process designed to uncover what we might call adjudicatory facts (who did what to whom) rather than legislative facts (whether a law is a good policy choice). So even if the goal is simply to get the right answer, the Court may do better in the ordinary case by deferring to the implicit legislative judgment as to the law's constitutionality than by trying to decide the question itself. It might adopt a doctrinal rule that says that the discrimination will be upheld if the legislature could rationally have thought that it produces net benefits to society.

What this deferential stance means is that the Court will basically accept the legislature's judgment. It will almost never strike down a law. If the legislature errs and enacts a law whose costs exceed its benefits, the doctrinal rule will nonetheless lead the Court to uphold the law. This deferential form of review, we could say, "underenforces" the Equal Protection Clause. As Figure 1 shows, underenforcing doctrine strikes down a good deal less than the Constitution actually prohibits, on the theory that leaving the legislature's judgment undisturbed will lead to fewer errors. That takes care of the ordinary case, and it leaves room for the Court to second-guess the legislature if things seem to have gone drastically wrong—if the legislature would be irrational to think the law was a good idea. But perhaps the Court can do better. Perhaps it can identify cases that are out of the ordinary, cases in which there are reasons to doubt that the legislature is acting in good faith. These reasons

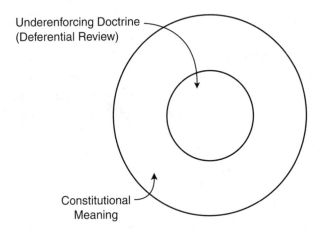

Figure 1. Underenforcing doctrine.

are factors that suggest that less deference is appropriate and that the legislative judgment should be treated more skeptically. The two I will consider here I call "the lessons of history" and "defects in democracy."

The Lessons of History

History might show that certain kinds of discrimination have frequently been used for improper purposes in the past. Discrimination against racial minorities, for instance, is an unfortunate staple of American history. It has frequently been the product of hostility, or of notions of racial hierarchy, that the Court is willing to declare illegitimate. This history justifies the Court in not deferring to the legislative judgment that such discrimination is innocent and in the public interest. Thus, the Court might evaluate the constitutionality of such discrimination without any deference to the legislature. It might attempt to balance costs and benefits itself; that is, it might adopt a non-deferential doctrinal rule that closely tracks the meaning of the Equal Protection Clause.

It might also go further. History shows that discrimination against racial minorities has so seldom, if ever, been used for a legitimate purpose that the Court might apply what it calls heightened scrutiny to the classification. Heightened scrutiny means that the Court adopts what I will call an anti-deferential doctrinal rule. This kind of rule not only refuses to accept the legislative judgment; it stacks the deck against the legislature. It does not simply ask whether the discrimination confers net benefits; instead, it requires that the discrimination be closely connected to a government interest of more than ordinary importance. (There are actually two different forms of heightened scrutiny, intermediate and strict, which I will discuss later. For present purposes, it is enough to distinguish between deferential doctrine and anti-deferential doctrine.)

Defects in Democracy

The second kind of situation in which an anti-deferential rule is justified is one in which structural problems make it likely that the legislature will fail to perform its cost-benefit balancing function accurately. An example of this sort of problem is a case in which the burdens of a law fall on out-of-staters, while its benefits go to residents. Out-of-staters cannot vote, so the legislature is unlikely to give full attention to burdens it imposes on them. It is likely to pass laws that burden them, that is, even if the benefits do not exceed the burdens. The same is true, to a lesser extent, of laws that burden politically weak

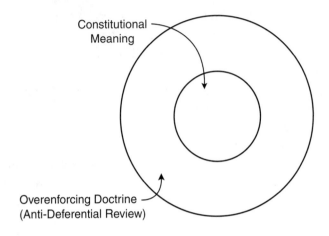

Figure 2. Overenforcing doctrine.

groups and benefit the politically powerful. Here again, non-deferential or anti-deferential doctrine makes sense.

While deferential doctrine underenforces the meaning of the Constitution, anti-deferential doctrine overenforces. As Figure 2 indicates, it strikes down more than the Constitution prohibits. It does so on the theory that some kinds of discrimination are so highly likely to be improper that the legislature should be allowed to use them only in extraordinary circumstances.

What our hypothetical Court has done so far is to decide that it will generally defer to state legislatures on equal protection questions, but to identify some circumstances in which greater skepticism is justified. The aim thus far has been to try to maximize the number of right answers. But there are other considerations that come into play. These are still more factors that may push the Court either to defer or not to defer.

The Costs of Error

The Court can make two kinds of mistakes. It can uphold laws that are in fact unconstitutional, and it can strike down laws that are constitutionally sound. The relative costs that it assigns to these errors will suggest more or less deference to the legislature. One aspect of the cost is the ease of correction. Here the two errors differ markedly. Upholding an unconstitutional law allows the government to burden an individual in a way that should not have been permitted. This is unfortunate, but if the problem is simply that the burdens of the law outweigh the benefits, it is likely in most circumstances that the legislature can fix the problem. That is, if a law turns out to have been a bad idea, it can be repealed.

If the Court errs in the other direction, by striking down a law it should have upheld, the cost is that the public is denied the benefits of that law, and the ability to govern itself democratically. In this case the fix is harder. The Court could reverse itself, but it is not fond of doing so and in any event the legislature is unlikely to re-enact a law that has been held unconstitutional. The only other possibility is a constitutional amendment, which is tremendously difficult to achieve.

The fact that a decision erroneously striking down a law is harder to correct than one erroneously upholding a law might suggest that deference to legislatures is generally appropriate. But the ease or difficulty of correction is not the only aspect of the cost of error. One also has to consider how harmful the errors are. The question here is the relative magnitude of the benefits to the public and the burdens on the affected individuals, and this analysis should probably be done on a case-by-case basis. To return to the Equal Protection Clause, if the discrimination takes the form of denying individuals something very important or valuable, its cost is greater. The Court might thus apply a non- or anti-deferential doctrinal rule to classifications that states make with respect to these very important interests, on the grounds that when such interests are at stake, the cost of erroneously upholding an unconstitutional deprivation is very high. It might be better, in such cases, to err on the side of protecting those interests. (Consider by way of comparison the oft-repeated maxim that it is better to let one hundred guilty people go free than to convict one innocent person, and the consequent adoption of the requirement that guilt be proven "beyond a reasonable doubt" in criminal trials.)

Thus far we have been concerned primarily with the effects of the Court's decisions on the parties to the case. But Supreme Court decisions have broader effects. The Supreme Court sits at the top of the hierarchy of federal courts, and on questions of federal law its decisions bind state courts as well. Furthermore, as authoritative statements of which governmental acts will be permitted and which will not, they play a significant role in shaping the behavior of both state and federal officials. The Court must therefore also consider how easy it is for lower courts and other government officials to understand and follow the rules it sets out. These considerations do not relate directly to the degree of deference the Court affords other actors; instead, they suggest that doctrine should take the form of a bright-line rule or a more vague and flexible standard.

Rules vs. Standards

The difference between rules and standards shapes the creation of doctrine in two primary ways. A rule has sharp edges; it permits or prohibits a definite range of action. A standard is more open-ended; its application in particular cases will be open to dispute. For example, the requirement that confessions be excluded from evidence unless police tell suspects that they have the right to remain silent is a rule. It is not a rule you will find in the Constitution, though. The Fifth Amendment prohibits the use of compelled confessions, but this prohibition on compulsion is a standard—what amounts to compulsion will depend on particular facts and circumstances.

The advantage of a rule over a standard is that when the Court announces a rule, other governmental actors can be relatively sure that they are complying with it. With a standard, they will not be sure until the Court decides the case. Lower courts will have a harder time accurately predicting what the Supreme Court would decide, and other officials will have doubts about whether the Court will uphold their actions. Thus, a desire for greater predictability and ease of compliance may lead the Court to create a doctrinal rule, even when the meaning of the Constitution is more like a standard. (And this, I will suggest, is what has happened with the Fifth Amendment and the *Miranda* warning.)

On the other hand, clear rules can also be undesirable precisely because of their clarity. If individuals know the rules that will be applied to assess their actions, they can shape their behavior around the rules. Government officials might be able to violate constitutional meaning while still honoring the Court's doctrine, or individuals might be able to claim shelter under the doctrine when the meaning left their conduct unprotected. An analogy is the practice of finding loopholes in the tax code, which ingenious lawyers regularly do, and to which Congress responds with regular amendments. The Supreme Court understandably does not want to generate constitutional doctrine that resembles the tax code, and still less to constantly monitor evasion and amend doctrine in response.

Thus, it might in some circumstances refuse to announce clear rules and keep its doctrine in the form of standards. (This factor, I will suggest, goes some way toward explaining the Court's current approach to state-sponsored religious exercises and displays.)

Thus far I have given an account of how a hypothetical Supreme Court might think. It is worth taking a moment to consider how it actually *does* think, or has thought in the past. That is, it is worth examining how closely actual equal protection doctrine resembles what a court would create if it were considering the factors I have listed.

The answer is that actual doctrine can be explained surprisingly well in terms of these factors. The fit is not perfect, and I will have something to say in later chapters about the cases in which doctrine diverges from what the factors would suggest. But as a general matter, the account I have given allows us to start with the constitutional meaning and to explain how the doctrine is derived from that meaning.

The meaning of the Equal Protection Clause, I have suggested, has two components. First, the government may never treat some people worse than others out of hostility. And second, whatever burden is inflicted on some group must be justified by a corresponding larger benefit to society. How has this constitutional meaning been translated into doctrine?

Equal protection doctrine works by asking two basic questions. First, what is the characteristic according to which the government treats people differently? And second, what does the differential treatment consist of? The different possible answers to these questions will lead the Court down different doctrinal paths, which are known as the tiers of scrutiny.

Under the first question, most answers will lead the Court to review the discrimination quite leniently. The Court will uphold most discriminatory governmental acts if they might rationally be thought to promote some legitimate state interest. That is, the court will not second-guess either the legislative motive or the legislature's implicit assessment of costs and benefits. This deferential posture, called "rational basis review," ends up leaving the responsibility for compliance with the Constitution primarily with the legislature. It might be that the classification is in fact motivated by hostility, or that the burdens it inflicts are greater than the benefits it produces. If either of those things is true, then the legislature has violated the Constitution. But the court will not interfere. Its doctrinal rule will lead it to uphold the discrimination. Rational basis review underenforces the Equal Protection Clause.

This deferential review is supported by a number of factors in most cases. The legislature is generally probably better than the Court at balancing costs and benefits. It is certainly better at knowing its own motive. These are examples of the institutional competence factor. Additionally, any errors the legislature might make are probably no more harmful than errors the Court would make, and the legislature's errors are easier to correct. These are examples of the cost of error factor.

When some or all of these factors are lacking, however, the Court's doctrinal rule changes. If the state is discriminating against women or against children born out of wedlock, the Court will apply a test called "intermediate scrutiny." Intermediate scrutiny requires that the discrimination be substantially related to an important governmental interest—it demands a more significant governmental end, and a tighter fit between means and end. Lesser deference can be justified on the grounds that women and illegitimate children are underrepresented in state legislatures. Thus, there are some grounds to think that legislatures might not weigh their interests appropriately. This is the factor of defects in democracy. Moreover, there is a history of discrimination against women and illegitimate children based on stereotypes now generally believed to be inaccurate. That history also suggests that legislatures are relatively likely to make mistakes about the preferences or characteristics of women and illegitimate children, which would throw off even a good-faith attempt to balance the costs and benefits of discrimination. This is the lessons of history factor.

Note, however, that the Court's doctrinal rule does not tell the Court to balance the costs and benefits itself, or to ask whether the discrimination is the product of improper motive. By demanding an important governmental interest and a relatively close means-end fit, it ensures that any discrimination that survives intermediate scrutiny will confer substantial benefits on society. But doctrine does not attempt to track meaning here, either. Discrimination based on improper motive will survive if it happens also to be substantially related to an important interest, and discrimination that is not based on improper motive and whose benefits outweigh its burdens will be held unconstitutional if it is not substantially related to an important interest.

Last, if the government is discriminating against a racial minority, or non-citizens, or if it is discriminating with respect to fundamental rights, the Court will employ what is known as "strict scrutiny." Strict scrutiny requires that the discrimination be necessary to serve a compelling state interest. Strict scrutiny is the Court's most demanding form of review. It does not defer to the legislature at all; indeed, the result of the application of strict scrutiny is almost always that the discrimination will be struck down.

As with intermediate scrutiny, a number of the factors

discussed earlier support the use of strict scrutiny in these contexts. As far as democratic defects are concerned, non-citizens cannot vote, so the legislature is likely to be relatively unresponsive to their concerns. Similarly, racial minorities frequently have lesser political power. The lessons of history come into play as well, for there is a substantial history of racial hostility expressed in laws that discriminate against racial minorities. With respect to fundamental rights, the primary factor is the costs of error. The Court might plausibly think that even if the legislature is likely to perform the cost-benefit analysis correctly, the consequences of allowing a mistake to survive are sufficiently severe that the Court's review should tilt against the possibility. (Again, the rule that guilt must be proved beyond a reasonable doubt is a useful comparison.)

Again, doctrine does not attempt to track meaning here. It might be the case that the legislature has discriminated against a racial minority without any hostility and that the benefits of the law exceed its burdens. (Historically, this has seldom happened, but it is certainly possible.) Nonetheless, the law will be struck down. Strict scrutiny will invalidate many discriminatory laws that do not conflict with the meaning of the Equal Protection Clause. On the other hand, it will allow very few laws that do conflict with the Equal Protection Clause to survive. Strict scrutiny overenforces the Equal Protection Clause.

The account I have given here of the tiers of scrutiny is what might be called a rational reconstruction of the doctrine. I have explained why the application of heightened scrutiny in certain contexts can be justified by reference to the factors I discussed earlier in this chapter. To use the terminology I will adopt in the next chapter, I have explained why this doctrine is legitimate. As we will see, the Court in fact applies heightened scrutiny in a somewhat wider variety of cases. Why it does so, and what sorts of justifications might be offered, are topics I will address later in the context of specific cases. But before I get to the cases, I return to the topic of legitimacy. The model of constitutional decision-making I have developed here is very different from the dichotomy between activism and direct enforcement favored by some politicians. And it is substantially different from the more plausible model of perfect enforcement that many people probably subscribe to. The next chapter demonstrates what the model means for the concepts of activism and legitimacy.

Further Reading

The basic idea that there is a significant difference between doctrine and meaning is fairly widely accepted among legal scholars. In the University of Virginia law review, I have offered a more technical exposition of the point, with applications similar to case studies in later chapters of this book, in *Constitutional Calcification: How the Law Becomes What the Court Does*, 91 Va. L. Rev. 1649 (2005). That article builds on earlier work by other scholars, notably Mitchell Berman's *Constitutional Decision Rules*, 90 Va. L. Rev. 1 (2004) and Richard Fallon's *Implementing the Constitution*, 110 Harv. L. Rev. 56 (1997). Fallon's article, slightly revised, is available in book form as *Implementing the Constitution* (Harvard University Press, 2001). Another similar and important contribution is Lawrence Sager's *Justice in Plainclothes: A Theory of American Constitutional Practice* (Yale University Press, 2004).

My discussion of the factors going into the creation of doctrine is heavily indebted to the ideas of John Hart Ely. Ely's *Democracy and Distrust* (Harvard University Press, 1980) should be read by any law student interested in constitutional law.

3

From Activism to Legitimacy

The basic question this book sets out to answer is how we can decide whether a particular judicial decision is legitimate. The distinction between legitimate and illegitimate decisions is meant to do what the concept of activism claims to do, but fails: to distinguish between decisions that should be accepted and those that should be condemned or opposed. What I mean by a legitimate decision is essentially an appropriate exercise of judicial authority. Citizens or government officials may disagree with a legitimate decision, but it provides no basis for charging that the judges have exceeded their proper role. The remedy for such decisions, if remedy is needed, is the ordinary appointments process.

Illegitimate decisions, by contrast, have something improper about them. They are not necessarily motivated by a judge's policy preferences—indeed, I will argue that the cause of most of the illegitimate decisions I will identify is a simple conceptual mistake. But an illegitimate decision provides grounds for criticism of the Court. A large number of illegitimate decisions, or a persistent series, might justify some of the drastic measures that the Court's current critics have proposed.

The key task, of course, is to come up with a test of legitimacy that is better than the obviously partisan rhetoric about plain meaning and activism. In order to help us figure out how to evaluate judicial decisions, I have started by explaining what judges actually do in constitutional cases. It would be understandable, however, if at this point you think that I have not helped at all. Evaluating judicial decisions would be very easy if the question was simply whether they were consistent with the "plain meaning" of the Constitution. I have argued, however, that the words of the Constitution alone seldom decide difficult cases. And it would still be relatively easy if the question was whether they were consistent with the meaning of the Constitution, even if that meaning is not so plain. I have argued, however, that in creating doctrine, the Court does not seek only to track the meaning of the Constitution, and for good reason.

These claims might seem only to make the task of evaluating decisions harder. To show that they are in fact steps toward a useful definition of legitimacy, I will take a moment here to recapitulate the structure of the argument. It starts with the observation that *judicial activism is an empty epithet.*

Judicial activism, as the concept is typically used, means deciding a case contrary to the plain meaning of the Constitution in order to promote the judge's political preferences. There have been attempts to offer other definitions, and these are worth considering. We might call a decision activist in a procedural sense, for instance, if the judge reaches out to decide issues that are not necessary to the resolution of the particular case. We might also call a decision activist if it strikes down a state or federal law. There the court is asserting itself against an elected branch of government; it is decreeing that some issue will not be settled through the democratic process.

Procedural activism is rare, however. This attempt to reformulate the concept will identify some of the decisions that should be questioned, but not all of them. It will not give us a general method of deciding whether decisions are legitimate or not.

Defining activism as striking down state or federal laws also has some merit. A judge who upholds a law can hardly be accused of imposing his views. A majority of the legislative members presumably shares those views, and if they change their mind, they can repeal the law. This definition of activism will tell us something about how aggressive the Court is with respect to other governmental actors, which is a relevant datum if we are trying to figure out whether the Court is abusing its authority. (The Rehnquist Court was quite aggressive, and if we accept this definition, that Court is fairly called the most activist in history.) But a decision that upholds a law is not always a good one. Some laws should be struck down, and since activism is generally taken to mean that a decision is illegitimate, this new definition will probably just lead to confusion.

So changing the definition of activism is not a solution. We should consider the concept on its own terms, as ignoring the plain meaning of the Constitution in favor of the judge's personal views. Defined this way, "activist" is just an insult. In practice, it turns out to mean nothing more or less than that the decision is inconsistent with the speaker's politics. The label "activist" turns out to possess exactly the same fault it claims to identify in judges: it is entirely result-oriented. This is so because *the plain meaning of the Constitution does not decide any difficult or controversial cases.*

For the concept of judicial activism to make sense, two

things must be true. First, determining the plain meaning of the Constitution must be relatively easy. Second, that plain meaning must tell judges how to decide individual cases.

The first proposition is indeed true. The Constitution is a remarkable document. The original Constitution set out the structure of the federal government in just over four thousand words. The amendments that have accrued over the years have added more, but the entire document can still be read easily in a sitting.

That is a stunning achievement. It is no exaggeration to say that there was genius at work in the writing of the Constitution. But the process by which the framers' proposal became our higher law is perhaps more remarkable still. The Constitution became effective upon ratification by conventions in nine states. The ratifiers were chosen through special elections. These elections were extraordinarily inclusive. Eight states relaxed their ordinary voter qualifications to allow participation by a broader selection of the citizenry; no state adopted more restrictive qualifications. The Constitution was, in a real sense, approved by that sovereign body invoked in its preamble: the People of the United States.

The framers may have been geniuses, but the ratifiers were not. They were, on the whole, ordinary citizens. The Constitution, as Franklin Roosevelt asserted, is "a layman's document, not a lawyer's contract," intended to be read and understood by citizens.[1] The *Federalist Papers*, the most comprehensive founding-era explanation and defense of the Constitution, were explicitly addressed not to any narrow elite but to the People of the State of New York. And it is the approval of the People that made the Constitution effective. It is their understanding of what was adopted, not that of the framers, that is significant. If ordinary citizens could understand the Constitution when it was drafted, they can understand it now.

The process will not necessarily be as easy as reading a contemporary newspaper. The Constitution contains some legal terms of art. "Bill of attainder," from Article I, is one; "due process of law," from the Fifth and Fourteenth Amendments, is another. Each invokes a series of decisions of English or American courts that have given substance and definition to otherwise obscure phrases. But such terms are few and far between. It will certainly help, in arriving at the understanding of the ratifiers, to have some knowledge of history, of what the concerns were that motivated the adoption of particular constitutional provisions. But the point of many constitutional provisions is relatively plain. "Equal protection of the laws," "the freedom of speech," "free exercise" of religion—the concepts to which these phrases refer are not mysterious. Take a straightforward understanding of the words and you will probably get pretty close to the thinking of the ratifiers. The meaning of a constitutional provision cannot be determined in an entirely objective manner, but it is something about which reasonable people can usually agree.

The problem, of course, is that this agreement takes place at a fairly high level of generality. And this is why the second proposition is false. Plain meaning does not tell judges how to decide any difficult cases. Deciding that the First Amendment prohibits government abridgment of the freedom of speech, for instance, tells us nothing about the hard questions of what counts as an abridgment (firing a government employee?), or even what counts as speech (art? dance? nude dance?). In fact, the kinds of people who talk about judicial activism tend to make very little effort to explain *how* a decision conflicts with plain meaning. Far more frequently, they simply assert that the conflict exists. As we have seen, this kind of assertion is generally wrong (the plain meaning of the Equal Protection Clause does not tell you which forms of discrimination are prohibited) and sometimes absurd (the plain meaning of the word "person" does include illegal aliens). In order to decide any but the most trivial cases, then, courts need something that takes them beyond the plain meaning of the Constitution. They need doctrine, and *doctrine is what decides cases.*

In order to decide whether to uphold or strike down some governmental act, the Supreme Court applies one of its doctrinal tests. The most common tests are the "tiers of scrutiny" mentioned in the preceding chapter's discussion of equal protection. They take the same basic form, requiring a particular kind of governmental interest and a particular fit between that interest and the law chosen as a means to achieve it. They differ with respect to the significance of the interest demanded—a legitimate interest will satisfy the most lenient review; an important interest is required to meet intermediate scrutiny, and a compelling interest is required for strict scrutiny. And they differ with respect to the tightness of the means-end fit the Court demands—a rational relationship between means and ends will satisfy "rational basis" review; intermediate scrutiny demands a substantial connection; and strict scrutiny requires that the act be necessary to serve the compelling interest.

These tests crop up repeatedly in different areas of constitutional law. They are not restatements or more precise specifications of the meaning of some particular provision of the Constitution. Indeed, applying these doctrinal tests will sometimes lead the Court to results that are *not* consistent with that meaning. That is, *doctrine diverges from meaning.*

Since doctrine is what does the work in Supreme Court decisions, evaluating those decisions boils down to evaluating the doctrine. (If the Court is drastically wrong about the meaning of the relevant constitutional provision, it can of course be faulted on that ground. But as my survey of cases will show, disagreements over meaning are in fact relatively rare.) But since doctrine does not, and is not intended to, precisely track the meaning of the Constitution, how can we evaluate it?

The answer to this question depends on the purpose of doctrine. As I argued in chapter 2, *doctrine primarily reflects the Court's decision to defer, or not to defer, to another governmental actor.*

Doctrine can, of course, get more complicated, and it can take forms other than the standard tiers of scrutiny. But at heart, most doctrine reflects the Court's judgment that another governmental actor can or cannot be relied upon to identify and observe constitutional limits on its behavior. That judgment is what we should be evaluating. This is so not only because that judgment frequently determines the outcome of cases. More important, if our concern is whether the Court is abusing its power and usurping the functions of other branches of government, as critics who call it "activist" charge, a lack of appropriate deference is the basic form such an abuse and usurpation would take.

The first part of this evaluation requires us to decide whether the Court is deferring. That part can be done objectively. When the Court applies rational basis review, it is deferring. When it applies strict scrutiny, it is not deferring; it has adopted what I called an anti-deferential stance. Even when the doctrinal test does not take the form of one of the tiers of scrutiny, it can usually be characterized as deferential, non-deferential, or anti-deferential. The key question, then, is whether the level of deference is appropriate. In answering that question, we are helped by the fact that *a relatively small number of factors determine the appropriate level of deference.*

In chapter 2, I identified five of these factors: institutional competence, defects in democracy, the costs of error, the lessons of history, and rules vs. standards. The list is not necessarily exhaustive, and other factors may come into play in some cases. The factors I identified are the ones I will use in evaluating the cases in subsequent chapters. My basic claim is that *decisions are legitimate if the level of deference the doctrine uses can be justified by reference to these factors.*

Whether a particular level of deference is justified by the presence or absence of particular factors is of course not a question that can be answered objectively. If there is no factor suggesting that the Court should defer, or conversely no reason to rely on the other governmental actor, the case may be relatively clear. But frequently there will be factors pointing in both directions.

Discrimination against women is a ready example. Weighing the costs and benefits of a discriminatory law is something the legislature can generally do better than courts, and to the extent that the balancing involves making policy, the basic idea of democracy is that the right policy choice is the one chosen by the people, even if the courts would make a "wiser" choice. The institutional competence factor suggests that courts should defer. On the other hand, women are underrepresented in state legislatures, which might suggest that defects in the democratic process would make a less deferential stance appropriate.

But the significance of the defects in democracy factor is not so clear. Even if women are underrepresented in legislatures, they are a majority of voters. If they acted in concert, they would be a dominant political force. And yet, even after women were guaranteed the vote by the Nineteenth Amendment in 1920, something still seemed to be going wrong. They were excluded from various professions and subjected to discriminatory treatment justified only by stereotypes about women's capabilities and appropriate roles. The lessons of history thus suggest that deference might not be appropriate.

Whether the Court should have adopted heightened scrutiny in response to this array of factors is a question with no clear right answer. There are arguments on each side, and neither is obviously correct. In such circumstances, we cannot test doctrine against any objective standards. Both choices are legitimate, for each is supported by some of the relevant factors. The question comes down to how we weigh the factors against each other, and that requires judgment, the inescapable essence of judging.

That is not to say that the model I have offered necessarily leads us to an impasse. By focusing attention on the relevant factors and their respective weight, it will produce both more frequent agreement and more constructive disagreement. An argument about the relative importance of history, voting rights, and the different competencies of courts and legislatures is one that can make some progress. Participants might be able to change each other's minds, or at least challenge each other to consider whether they attach the same significance to the same factors in other contexts (such as, perhaps, affirmative action, where the factors supporting judicial deference are stronger). It is, at any rate, substantially better than the empty name-calling that accusations of "activism" amount to.

In the remainder of this book, I will apply the method of analysis I have set out here: I will analyze cases by starting with the meaning of the relevant constitutional provision and asking whether the Court's choice of doctrine reflects an appropriate level of deference. I hope that the method will prove its worth in that analysis and that readers will find it a useful way of thinking about the legitimacy of Supreme Court decisions. Before I begin, however, I pause to address an objection that has doubtless already occurred to some readers.

My claim that we should be concerned primarily with the legitimacy of doctrine assumes that doctrine is necessary to decide cases. I have argued that this is true because the plain meaning of the Constitution, by itself, does not allow judges to reach decisions in specific cases. Having decided that the Equal Protection Clause prohibits unjustified discrimination, for instance, a court still needs to decide whether a particular discriminatory law is justified or not. In making that decision, the court will need to decide how much deference to give to the legislature's balancing of costs and benefits—it will need to apply some doctrinal rule embodying a deferential, non-deferential, or anti-deferential stance.

Some people, including prominent academics and Supreme Court justices, think that there is another way to reach a decision. Rather than asking whether the legislature can be trusted to balance costs and benefits accurately, proponents of the school of constitutional interpretation called originalism argue that we should ask whether the people who ratified the Equal Protection Clause would have thought the discriminatory law was justified. They claim that supplementing the words of the Constitution with historical evidence about how the ratifiers believed they applied to particular circumstances will allow judges to get from the general meaning of a phrase like "equal protection" to a decision in an individual case.

This is not an enterprise that requires the balancing of competing values, or an assessment of the functioning of the democratic process. Rather, it is a historical inquiry focused on what people thought at the time of ratification. Consequently, there is no need to adopt a doctrinal structure that sets an appropriate level of judicial deference to legislative determinations. Unsurprisingly, originalists tend to be skeptical of doctrine. They believe that relatively clear right answers to specific constitutional questions exist, and that the appropriate role of courts is simply to enforce those right answers. Originalism, that is, embraces the idea of perfect enforcement, which I have said is a fallacy. It presents a challenge to the model I have set out, and it is therefore worth discussing in some detail.

Originalism and the Living Constitution

In modern constitutional theory, originalism sets itself against the interpretive practice known as living constitutionalism, which gives greater priority to contemporary understandings. The debate between originalists and living constitutionalists is generally considered one of the most important current battles over how the Constitution should be interpreted. In what follows, I will briefly set out the debate and then explain why I think its significance is drastically overstated.

The standard argument for originalism is relatively straightforward. The Constitution, recall, gets its legal effectiveness from the approval of the ratifiers. When the original Constitution was ratified, and when amendments were added to it over the course of years, a particular meaning was enacted, and judges are not given the authority to change that meaning. The role of a judge is to say what the Constitution *does* mean, not what it ought to mean; if change is needed, Article V sets out the procedure by which it can be amended. Allowing judges free rein to change the meaning of the Constitution to suit the perceived needs of the day takes sovereignty away from the American people and places it in the hands of an unelected judiciary. Adherence to original understanding, by contrast, prevents judges from imposing their own values.

Originalists thus argue that constitutional cases should be decided according to our best guess as to how the ratifiers would have decided them. Judges should protect a right to abortion only if the ratifiers would have agreed that it existed; if the ratifiers believed that racially segregated schools were consistent with the Equal Protection Clause, then judges should not interfere. Anything else, originalists say, is illegitimate (or even "activist").

The conventional argument for the living Constitution focuses on the fact that conditions and attitudes have changed greatly since the framers' times. Living constitutionalists argue that the Constitution must be able to adapt to respond to current needs and problems rather than remaining frozen in time. Because the amendment process is so difficult and cumbersome, requiring a two-thirds majority in both the House and the Senate and then ratification by the legislatures of three-quarters of the states, living constitutionalists seem to view judicial modification of the Constitution with equanimity—a necessary evil, at the worst. Without judicial changes, they say, states would still be allowed to segregate schools, ban interracial marriage, and exclude women from the practice of law, to give just a few prominent examples.

When the argument is viewed in these terms, it seems fairly clear that the originalists have the better of it. The Constitution as written may not be perfect, but what is the point of a written Constitution at all if judges have the freedom to modify it as they see fit? And what reason is there to think that judges will write a better Constitution than the one we have?

As Justice Antonin Scalia is fond of pointing out, judges might as well decide to disregard individual rights provisions as to expand them. That is, although originalists tend to be political conservatives and living constitutionalists political liberals, there is no reason to think that judges would consistently modify the Constitution in a liberal direction. In speeches, Justice Scalia has gone so far as to say that one would have to be "an idiot" to believe in the living Constitution. And if the descriptions I have given of originalism and the living Constitution were accurate, he might well be right.

But things are not that simple. Originalism is not quite all it claims to be, in part because the precise understandings it seeks to enforce are frequently imaginary. The understanding of the ratifiers, in many cases, probably did not go beyond the vague or general plain meaning; that is, the ratifiers would have disagreed among themselves as to how specific cases should be decided.

Consider, for instance, the question of whether the Necessary and Proper Clause, which allows Congress to pass laws necessary and proper to implement the powers granted to it by Article I, permits the creation of a federal bank. This was one of the big disputes of the framing era, and it divided the framers themselves. Alexander Hamilton argued that the bank was constitutionally allowed, while James Madison asserted that it was not. If Hamilton and Madison—who were both present at the Constitutional Convention and who had collaborated on the Federalist Papers—could not agree, what are the odds that the ratifiers had a clear and uniform understanding on this question?

For a more recent example, consider the Equal Rights Amendment. The ERA was submitted to the states for consideration by Congress in 1972 but never ratified. Section 1 of the

ERA provided that "Equality of rights under the law shall not be denied or abridged by the United States or by any State on account of sex." This is, of course, very much like the Equal Protection Clause, except that it focuses specifically on sex discrimination. (One of the reasons it failed to achieve ratification, ironically, may have been the Supreme Court's contemporaneous use of the Equal Protection Clause itself to forbid sex discrimination.) How clear and consistent were the contemporary understandings of its meaning for specific cases?

Not very. Supporters and opponents clashed over a number of issues—whether sex-segregated bathrooms would become unconstitutional, whether the ERA would require that women be drafted into combat, and even whether it would require states to permit same-sex marriage. Harvard law professor Paul Freund, a widely respected constitutional authority, testified to a Senate subcommittee that this last consequence would indeed result: "If the law must be as undiscriminating concerning sex as it is toward race, it would follow that laws outlawing wedlock between members of the same sex would be as invalid as laws forbidding miscegenation."[2]

On the other hand, it seems unlikely that the concern for women's equality that inspired the ERA is necessarily connected to approval of same-sex marriage, so the drafters might have had a different view. The ERA never gained the required thirty-eight state ratifications, so courts never had to grapple with these issues. But the debate over them suggests that the consequences of the ERA were less than entirely clear to the drafters and potential ratifiers.

The existence of this sort of disagreement suggests that originalism will not deliver clearly correct answers in many cases. This is not simply a practical problem. Originalists like to claim that adherence to original meaning prevents judges from imposing their own values, while living constitutionalism does not. But if the ratifiers would not have agreed on how specific cases should be decided, the supposed constraint is illusory. That is, a judge following an originalist methodology could still reach whatever results he wanted by highlighting some historical evidence and downplaying the rest. So originalism, as a methodology, does not in fact prevent judges from imposing their preferences on society. Historical evidence does not do much more than "plain meaning" as far as deciding difficult cases goes.

Still, if the choice is between plain meaning plus history and judicial whim alone, originalism may be the better option. My broader claim here is that the conventional way of framing the debate is deeply misleading.

It is misleading because the argument I gave for originalism makes a fundamental error. It assumes that if constitutional *meaning* remains the same, then the outcomes of cases must remain the same, even as surrounding facts and circumstances change.

Living constitutionalists and originalists share this assumption, but it is easy to demonstrate that they are both wrong. Imagine for a moment that the Constitution had a clause it does not—a clause providing that senators, while engaged in debate, "shall wear the latest Fashions." This clause would, quite clearly, direct one thing in 1789 and another now. Conduct that the ratifiers deemed consistent with the clause—dressing in knee breeches and a powdered wig—would be inconsistent with today's understanding of the language. Should an originalist judge, exercising fidelity to the ratifiers' understanding, hold that senators must dress according to the fashions of the eighteenth century?

The answer is obviously no. The ratifiers of a clause requiring "the latest Fashions" plainly expected the set of activities permitted by that clause to change over time. The word "latest" is a dead giveaway. Still, even if the clause just required "fashionable Attire," it would be reasonable to think that the ratifiers intended its requirements to change. A provision that required senators to adhere to the ratifiers' understanding of what was fashionable would be a rather foolish one. It would be easy to see, at the time of ratification, that such a provision would quickly lose its fit and fail to serve the intended purpose. Requiring twentieth-century senators to dress in eighteenth-century costumes would make them look not fashionable but ridiculous. In adjusting the outcome of cases to follow the evolution of fashion, a judge would not be engaged in modifying constitutional meaning. She would be following the original understanding—an understanding that clothes that seemed fashionable in 1789 would appear anachronistic and silly centuries later, and that the purpose of ensuring fashionable senators requires reference to future notions of fashion.

So it is clearly possible to write constitutional provisions that direct different outcomes as times change. To put the point in the terminology I shall use for the rest of this discussion, it is possible for the *meaning* of a constitutional provision to remain constant while its *applications* change. Most originalists ignore this possibility; they are what we could call "application originalists" rather than "meaning originalists." But the possibility does exist. The question, once we have established this initial point, is which, if any, of the provisions in our actual Constitution fit that description.

One way to do this would be simply to look at the language. Some words, like "latest," clearly announce that their range of application is to be flexible. Others, like "thirty-five," suggest that their applications are meant to be fixed.

If we look through the Constitution, we will certainly find some words that suggest flexibility. "Unreasonable" searches and seizures are prohibited by the Fourth Amendment, "speedy" trial guaranteed by the Sixth, and "excessive bail" and "cruel and unusual punishment" forbidden by the Eighth. The possibility of concealing a lethal handgun in a pocket might make reasonable searches that would have been considered unreasonable by the framers. The available means of transportation for judge, jury, and accused might bear on what counts as a "speedy" trial. An inquiry into "excessive" bail might take inflation into account, and whether a punishment is "unusual" might depend on whether it is common now, not whether it was in 1791 when the Eighth Amendment was ratified.

We should not, however, focus solely on the words of the Constitution, for it is semantically possible that these terms incorporate by reference not current circumstances but those of the ratifiers' times. The appropriate inquiry looks to the words and also to the purpose of the relevant constitutional provision, asking whether that purpose is better served by a static or a flexible range of applications.

Each of the provisions I have mentioned probably better serves the purpose the ratifiers intended if its range of applications is flexible. A Fourth Amendment that banned police from patting down suspects would expose them to serious danger; it would no longer strike a sensible balance between individual privacy and public safety. A Sixth Amendment speedy trial guarantee that was keyed to travel by horseback would make little sense in the modern world; it would allow authorities to impose arbitrary delays. A prohibition on excessive bail expressed in 1791 dollars would set an absurdly low threshold in the twenty-first century; it would make bail requirements meaningless. And defining "cruel and unusual punishments" by reference to 1791 understandings and practices would allow punishments that have now become rare or nonexistent because they were deemed barbaric and inhumane.

Those examples are relatively minor, though the proper interpretation of the Cruel and Unusual Punishment Clause has been a matter of some dispute in cases I will discuss later. The Equal Protection Clause is an issue of greater significance, in part because the changes that judges might take into account include changes in values as well as facts. Changes in values are relevant because a prohibition on unjustified discrimination is value-laden. There is no objective and timeless standard by which to determine whether discrimination is justified, not even the cost-benefit analysis I offered earlier, for costs and benefits depend on attitudes as well as material facts. And even those who accept the idea of a reasonableness standard that takes changing facts into account in evaluating Fourth Amendment searches and seizures might argue that changes in societal values should not be allowed to change the outcome of constitutional cases.

But the line between facts and values is not as clear or as sharp as it might seem, for value judgments about the justifiability of discrimination may depend on background factual beliefs and assumptions. We can see this by considering a few examples of practices that the ratifiers believed were acceptable, but that modern Americans do not. The historical evidence strongly suggests that the ratifiers of the Equal Protection Clause did not believe that it would stop states from segregating schools, or banning interracial marriage, or excluding women from the practice of law.

Why would anyone think these things—some of which seem obviously unjustified to modern sensibilities—were constitutionally unproblematic? Until relatively recently, many "facts" justified these forms of discrimination. Interracial marriage was considered likely either to produce monsters or at the least to compromise the purity of the white gene pool. Educating black and white children together probably seemed simply impossible; as Abraham Lincoln put it in 1858, "[t]here is a physical difference between the white and black races which I believe will forever forbid the two races living together on terms of social and political equality."[3] And as for women lawyers, as Justice Joseph Bradley wrote in *Bradwell v. Illinois,* five years after the ratification of the Fourteenth Amendment, "the natural timidity and delicacy of the female evidently unfits her for many of the occupations of civil life."

Additionally, discrimination was considered justified as a reflection of the natural order of things, a conclusion often couched in religious terms. Justice Bradley rested his assertion that "[t]he paramount destiny and mission of woman are to fulfill the noble and benign offices of wife and mother" on the simple ground that "[t]his is the law of the Creator."[4] And the trial court judge who enforced Virginia's ban on interracial marriages against Mildred Jeter and Richard Loving observed that "Almighty God created the races white, black, yellow, malay and red, and he placed them on separate continents. . . . The fact that he separated the races shows that he did not intend for the races to mix."[5] These rationales may once have been sufficiently widely accepted to count as adequate justification for discrimination; they may once have seemed like common sense. But they no longer appear that way. A modern legislature would be unlikely to rely on them in enacting a law, and a modern judge would be less likely still to accept them as justification.

If the ratifiers' beliefs about the likely applications of the Equal Protection Clause depend on facts that are now deemed false and on beliefs about the nature of the world that are no longer shared, working in concert to produce attitudes that now seem reprehensible, what is a court to do? It could attempt to enforce those attitudes despite the fact that they command results now clearly at odds with an ordinary understanding of the constitutional language. That is what application original-ism would require. But a sensible originalism—what I call *meaning originalism*—does not require such results, and their perversity is itself a suggestion that application originalism is not the right way to proceed.

Living constitutionalists sometimes argue that original-ism should be rejected because it would allow practices we now think are unjust. That is a result-oriented argument, and it is not very convincing. It boils down to the proposition that we should read the Constitution to mean what we want it to mean. What I am suggesting here is somewhat different. It is that reading the Equal Protection Clause to contain a fixed set of applications will predictably lead to results that future gen-erations will find outrageous. And because fixed applications lead to those results, it is more sensible to suppose that the ratifiers understood and intended the applications to be flex-ible. Meaning originalism suggests that the Equal Protection Clause is one of those provisions whose applications change while its meaning remains constant.

This approach is consistent with the words of the Con-stitution. The Equal Protection Clause cannot be read as set-ting out a clear rule that all forms of discrimination are pro-hibited. It must allow state universities to favor students with higher grades and test scores; it must allow states to impose age and vision restrictions on drivers. What it prohibits is unjusti-fied discrimination, and justification can certainly be assessed according to modern standards as easily—perhaps more easily—as to those of 1868. (It may be, as originalists frequently claim, that judges are not especially good at figuring out what modern societal values are, but why then should they be considered good at figuring out what those values were over a hundred years ago?)

It also, I believe, does a better job of fulfilling the purpose that the ratifiers had in mind for the Equal Protection Clause. The clause was adopted in the wake of the Civil War, and it was clearly intended to stop states from discriminating against the newly freed slaves. But it was intended to do more than that. The drafters considered and rejected language that would have prohibited only discrimination based on race, and they considered and rejected language that would have prohibited only discrimination with respect to particular rights. Their purpose seems to have been more general; it seems to have been to stop states from discriminating in ways that a national majority found unjustified.

So the key question is whether this purpose is better served by a fixed or flexible range of applications. The answer is that only a flexible one can ensure the continued priority of national values. A ban on only those forms of discrimination that the ratifiers thought were unjustified will soon lose fit. The discriminatory practices the ratifiers focused on will lose their practical significance, and new ones will take their place. If equal protection is to continue to protect, it must be able to meet the challenge of new discrimination. Employing current standards to assess justification does just that. It allows an emerging national consensus to override discrimination that was accepted in the past. By so doing, it ensures that vulnerable minorities will continue to be protected against treatment that local majorities find acceptable but national majorities do not. Since the words of the Equal Protection Clause do not limit its application to particular issues or forms of discrimination, it makes sense to assume that this form of protection was what the drafters and ratifiers intended. If this understanding of equal protection is correct, then meaning originalism does not present a challenge to the model I have set out. If applications are to be assessed from a contemporary perspective, then the resolution of equal protection questions will require consideration of contemporary facts and values, and courts will be required to decide the appropriate level of deference to afford the judgments of other governmental actors. That is, meaning originalism requires courts to construct doctrine in the way I have described.

Legitimacy Reassessed

Thus far I have argued that two common understandings of what counts as justified constitutional decision-making are incorrect. Political rhetoric suggests that judges should enforce the plain meaning of the Constitution. Anything else is activism.

The problem with this idea of direct enforcement is that it is obviously unworkable. The plain meaning of the Constitution simply does not give judges sufficient guidance to decide concrete cases. Because answers in many cases are not clear, and may depend on matters legislatures can handle better than courts, I argue that doctrine is needed to mediate between the Constitution and specific decisions.

A somewhat more sophisticated understanding, of which application originalism is one variant, offers a different challenge to the legitimacy of doctrine. It suggests that judges should decide all cases as the ratifiers of the Constitution would have expected. Figuring out what these expectations were may be difficult, but it is emphatically a judicial task, and there is no need to balance interests or consider the judgments of other actors. Anything but enforcing historically right answers, again, is activism.

The problem with this understanding is that it is likely that many constitutional provisions were intended to have applications that changed with time and circumstance. If that is so, right answers will depend on determinations that legislatures are frequently better than courts at making. Once again, the key question for courts will not be a narrow legal or historical one about the meaning of the Constitution or the understanding of the ratifiers. It will be about how much deference is appropriately given to the legislature.

The construction of doctrine, as I have described it, is largely driven by this question. With few exceptions, the factors I discussed in chapter 2 relate to the extent to which the Court should be willing to second-guess legislative judgments. For instance, a history of constitutional violations suggests less deference, as does a predictable malfunction in the representative process; on the other hand, the existence of a complicated factual or policy question suggests more.

Legitimacy of doctrine, I argue, is thus best evaluated by considering whether the doctrine responds sensibly to the presence or absence of these factors. This standard allows us a clear view of whether the Supreme Court is performing its role appropriately. The second part of this book takes that standard and applies it to Supreme Court decisions—some that I think are right, some that I think are wrong, and some that everyone agrees are indefensible. From the perspective I have developed, we will be able to see why some controversial decisions make sense, and what went wrong in those that do not. We will be able to see how some areas of doctrine might be improved.

And, in the last part of the book, we will see whether the Supreme Court deserves the criticism it has absorbed of late.

Further Reading

For further development of the concern that Supreme Court decisions are making the Constitution inaccessible to ordinary citizens, see Joseph Goldstein, *The Intelligible Constitution* (Oxford University Press, 1995). For a word-by-word reading of the Constitution, see Akhil Amar's remarkable *America's Constitution: A Biography* (Random House, 2005). For the debate over originalism and the living Constitution, an excellent resource is Antonin Scalia, *A Matter of Interpretation: Federal Courts and the Law* (Princeton University Press, 1997). That book offers Scalia's statement of his originalist methodology and commentary from some notable legal scholars. Ronald Dworkin's response is in many ways similar to the one I offer here, though Dworkin seems to place a greater emphasis on the ability of judges to apply a philosophical methodology to determine the "true" meaning of concepts such as liberty and equality, whereas I suggest a more modest role of reflecting societal values. Dworkin's position is developed more fully in *Freedom's Law: The Moral Reading of the American Constitution* (Harvard University Press, 1996). A similar view, couched in philosophical terms, is advanced by Christopher Green in *Originalism and the Sense-Reference Distinction*, in the 2005 volume of the St. Louis Law Journal. Also worth reading is Randy Barnett's originalist argument for a more libertarian understanding of the Constitution, *Restoring the Lost Constitution: The Presumption of Liberty* (Princeton University Press 2005). Justice Stephen Breyer has recently offered a statement of his approach to constitutional interpretation, which rejects originalism in favor of more pragmatic considerations, in *Active Liberty: Interpreting Our Democratic Constitution* (Knopf, 2005). An excellent discussion of the circumstances surrounding the drafting and ratification of the Fourteenth Amendment, and what light that history sheds on its meaning, can be found in William E. Nelson, *The Fourteenth Amendment: From Political Principle to Judicial Doctrine* (Harvard University Press, 1988).

II
Easy Cases

Part I set out the terms on which I think Supreme Court doctrine and decisions should be evaluated. The following parts of the book proceed to the evaluation of specific cases. Some of the cases I will discuss are recent, while others are quite old. Some are well known even among non-lawyers, and some are not. Some are considered right, so clearly right that a constitutional theory discredits itself with the suggestion that they are wrongly decided. Some are so universally condemned that the reverse is true: a theory of constitutional interpretation must explain why they are wrong. But they are all important, and if you want to decide whether the Supreme Court has done a good job, they are the data that should be analyzed.

4

Equal Protection, Criminal Procedure, Executive Detention

I begin with the cases that I find easy, and the first two are cases that almost everyone agrees are right, the ones that have become the fixed stars of our constitutional jurisprudence. I start, that is, with *Brown v. Board of Education* and *Loving v. Virginia.*

Equal Protection: *Brown* and *Loving*

BROWN v. BOARD OF EDUCATION

As most people know, the Supreme Court's 1954 decision in *Brown v. Board of Education* held that racial segregation of public schools violated the Equal Protection Clause of the Fourteenth Amendment.[1] The Court's opinion, written by Chief Justice Earl Warren, worked in two steps. First, the Court considered the historical question of the original understanding of the Equal Protection Clause. The Court's actions had suggested that it deemed this question central to the case. After the initial argument in 1952 the Court ordered another round of argument and briefing focusing on the original understanding.

In the actual decision, however, the Court gave the original understanding short shrift. The historical data was unclear, Warren pronounced, and in any event the Court could not "turn the clock back to 1868."[2] Facts and circumstances, including the nature and significance of public education, had changed. Instead, the Court proceeded straight to the question of whether racially segregated educational facilities could be equal within the meaning of the Equal Protection Clause: that is, assuming that the black and white schools were of equal quality, did the mere fact of segregation violate equal protection?

The Court's affirmative answer relied on the theory that segregation by its nature inflicted harms on black children. "To separate them from others of similar age and qualifications solely because of their race generates a feeling of inferiority as to their status in the community that may affect their hearts and minds in a way unlikely ever to be undone."[3] It supported this theory with a reference to social science literature, including a study finding that black children in segregated schools allowed to select between white and black dolls exhibited a preference for the white. "[I]n the field of public education," Warren concluded, "the doctrine of 'separate but equal' has no place. Separate educational facilities are inherently unequal."[4]

Brown's reception by legal scholars was decidedly cool. There was, of course, widespread endorsement of the decision by liberals. But even among *Brown* enthusiasts, the praise was directed more toward the result than the reasoning. The *New*

York Times editorial board praised the Court as "the guardian of our national conscience,"[5] and the *St. Louis Post-Dispatch* lauded *Brown* as "a great and just act of judicial statesmanship."[6] Neither of these comments suggested much enthusiasm for Warren's judicial craftsmanship. Columbia law professor Herbert Wechsler offered a typical academic view in a speech at Harvard Law School, observing that while he "should like to think" that there existed a convincing legal rationale for the decision, "I have not yet written the opinion."[7]

Among those who did not favor the result as a matter of politics, the reaction was less polite skepticism than fury. The Southern Manifesto decried *Brown* as a substitution of the justices' "personal political and social ideas for the established law of the land" and vowed to "use all lawful means to bring about the reversal of this decision which is contrary to the Constitution."[8] Individual southern political leaders used stronger language. Senator James Eastland of Mississippi called *Brown* a "legislative decision by a political court"; Governor Herman Talmadge of Georgia charged that the justices "had blatantly ignored all law and precedent."[9]

Other opponents declined to stay within the bounds of the law. In 1963, after federal troops had forcibly integrated Alabama schools, facing down Governor George Wallace and the state militia, Klansmen bombed a Baptist church in Birmingham. Northern whites, many of whom had been relatively uninterested in the civil rights movement, reacted with horror to the bombing and to subsequent attacks on civil rights marchers. Indeed, law professor Michael Klarman suggests that *Brown*'s greatest contribution to racial equality was not any constitutional principle but rather its effect in driving segregationists to violence, delegitimizing their position before a national audience.[10]

Nowadays, those willing to argue that *Brown* was wrongly decided are far fewer. Some originalists still take the position that *Brown* exemplifies illegitimate judicial decision-making in the name of a desirable result.[11] But most originalists are more concerned to explain how *Brown* is actually correct on originalist grounds, thinking (rightly) that an approach to constitutional interpretation under which *Brown* was wrongly decided will have little appeal for the American public.[12]

But was *Brown* right in terms of constitutional meaning? From the perspective of application originalism, the answer is probably no. The Congress that drafted the Fourteenth Amendment was itself running a segregated school system in the District of Columbia, and in 1868 integrated schooling would likely have seemed so impractical that the Constitution could not possibly command it. But I have already said that application originalism is a misguided approach to constitutional interpretation, and the Equal Protection Clause is one of the constitutional provisions that a meaning originalist would likely understand as having a flexible range of applications.

Granting that point, *Brown* becomes quite easy. Almost immediately after the Fourteenth Amendment was ratified, the Court was using it to strike down state laws that affixed "a brand of inferiority."[13] Segregated schooling violates the Fourteenth Amendment not because of any psychological effects on children—indeed, the studies on which *Brown* relied are notoriously inconclusive—but because it is a state-sponsored attempt to create an inferior class of citizens. The Supreme Court was not always willing to admit this fact, and the *Brown* opinion carefully avoids asserting it, in keeping with Warren's aspiration to write an opinion that was "above all non-accusatory."[14] But the truth is that racial segregation in schooling was part of a widespread and consistent state attempt to create and maintain a racial caste system. That is quite obviously not equal.

To say that racially segregated schooling violates the Equal Protection Clause is not quite the same thing as saying that a court should strike it down. That is the point of my distinction between doctrine and meaning. So a question remains whether the Court should have crafted doctrinal rules that would have led it to uphold segregation even if it felt that the practice violated the meaning of the Constitution.

This question, too, is quite easy. Arguing that a court is better than a legislature at assessing the costs and benefits of segregated schooling might indeed be difficult. (It is perhaps for this reason that the Court turned to the social science literature.) But arguing that Southern legislatures could not be trusted to make impartial decisions about racial classifications in the 1950s is not hard at all. Segregation in the South, as Charles Black put it, "comes down in apostolic succession from slavery and the *Dred Scott* case."[15] A doctrinal rule that essentially takes away from the legislature the power to use racial classifications against racial minorities makes a good deal of sense. It is supported by the lessons of history and also by the fact that Southern legislatures were likely not to give equal weight to the interests of their black constituents.

That is exactly what modern doctrine does: it imposes a test that discrimination against racial minorities will almost never be able to satisfy. Equal protection doctrine had not quite assumed its present form at the time of *Brown*, but under then-existing doctrine, the decision would have been the same. Warren's opinion actually avoided doctrine, in the hopes of producing something that was "short [and] readable by the lay public."[16] But the Supreme Court itself evidently understood *Brown* as resting on some principle about the inherent unconstitutionality of segregation, not the specifics of doll studies. In subsequent cases, it extended *Brown* to order the desegregation of public golf courses and swimming pools, without any explanation of how the sociological data of *Brown* was relevant to those contexts. Indeed, it did so by unsigned order, without issuing any opinions at all. Like *Brown*, those decisions are both correct as a matter of constitutional meaning and consistent with sensible doctrine.

LOVING v. VIRGINIA

In 1958, two Virginia residents named Mildred Jeter and Richard Loving were married in the District of Columbia. Shortly thereafter, they returned to Virginia. This would have been unremarkable except for one fact: Richard Loving was white, and Mildred Jeter was black. Their interracial marriage violated Virginia's Racial Integrity Act, and they were convicted and sentenced to one year in prison. The trial judge suspended the sentence for twenty-five years on the condition that they leave the state of Virginia and not return together for twenty-five years.

By the time the Supreme Court heard the case in 1967, equal protection doctrine had progressed further toward its modern form. Racial classifications, the Court wrote, were subject to a "very heavy burden of justification."[17] The Court would not defer to the legislature's judgment as to the desirability of racial discrimination but rather would require it to show that the discrimination advanced a very important goal.

Virginia failed that task utterly. The trial court that sentenced the Lovings had relied on the fact that "Almighty God created the races [and] he did not intend for the races to mix"—a controversial religious rationale that would not meet even a lesser standard of scrutiny. The Virginia Supreme Court incorporated by reference its assertions in an earlier case that "the State's legitimate purposes were 'to preserve the racial integrity of its citizens,' and to prevent 'the corruption of blood,' 'a mongrel breed of citizens,' and 'the obliteration of racial pride.'"[18] The first three of these justifications, though widely accepted when the Racial Integrity Act was adopted in 1924, had come to seem false by 1967: racist science was increasingly discredited. The last the Supreme Court characterized as "obviously an endorsement of the doctrine of White Supremacy"[19]—not merely an inadequate justification but a potentially invalidating one. In its briefs before the Court, the state asserted merely that on the question of interracial children, "the scientific evidence is substantially in doubt"[20] and asked for deference to the legislature.

As did *Brown*, *Loving* presented a situation where the state's actions clearly violated the meaning of the Constitution because they attempted to promote and perpetuate a racial caste system. Any doctrinal test other than an extraordinarily deferential one would have struck them down. The doctrine that the Court had developed to assist it in dealing with discrimination against racial minorities was leading it instead toward an anti-deferential doctrinal test, which made the result even easier. Additionally, in *Loving* the Court was dealing with deprivation of the right to marry, something it characterized as a "fundamental freedom" and one of the "vital personal rights."[21] The high cost of such a deprivation also justifies a less deferential stance toward the legislature. Thus, like *Brown*, *Loving* is easily correct in terms of both meaning and doctrine.

Criminal Procedure: *Miranda* and *Dickerson*

Brown and *Loving* deal with discrimination against a minority that has been subject to a history of unjustified treatment. They are easy cases, for the practices they strike down are at the core of what the Equal Protection Clause sought to eradicate. Other equal protection cases are harder, and I will deal with them later. But I have spent a lot of time discussing equal protection, and it is time now to look at some other areas of law to see how the evaluative process I have described works with them.

MIRANDA v. ARIZONA

Miranda v. Arizona, decided in 1966, is almost as famous as *Brown,* though it has never achieved the same iconic status.[22] In *Miranda,* the Court ruled that in order to use a suspect's confession in a subsequent prosecution, police had to administer the famous *Miranda* warning. The warning, now well known to any television viewer, begins, "You have the right to remain silent. Anything you say can be used against you in a court of law." It goes on to explain the availability of a lawyer and the right to have a lawyer present during questioning.

Miranda was immediately attacked by conservatives as an example of judicial activism and undue sympathy for criminal defendants. If the question is whether the *Miranda* rule is part of the meaning of the Constitution, the attacks are fully justified. The constitutional provision at issue in *Miranda* was the Fifth Amendment's Self-Incrimination Clause, which provides that no person "shall be compelled in any criminal case to be a witness against himself." This does not simply mean that a person cannot be forced to testify against himself in court. Testimony may be given in out-of-court statements, and the principle that a compelled confession cannot be used in court follows quite easily from the words of the Self-Incrimination Clause.

What does not follow is the *Miranda* warning. Obviously the Constitution does not contain those familiar words. More significantly, application of the *Miranda* test prevents prose-cutors from using many confessions that are entirely volun-tary, if police fail to give the warning. *Miranda,* then, gets lots of cases "wrong" as a matter of constitutional meaning: the doctrine prohibits some things that the Constitution itself does not.

That makes it a less obviously legitimate decision than *Brown* or *Loving.* But doctrine can be legitimate even if it goes beyond the meaning of the Constitution. The question is whether the doctrine that the Court has crafted can be justi-fied. The justification for *Miranda* is readily apparent: it has to do with the relative virtues of rules and standards.

The Fifth Amendment's Self-Incrimination Clause en-acts a standard. Whether a confession is voluntary is not a question that can be decided mechanically. It requires con-sideration of a wide range of factors. Before *Miranda,* the doc-trinal test had called on courts to make the decision by con-sidering the "totality of circumstances." This approach had a number of defects. It gave little guidance to police, who were left uncertain as to how far they could go in eliciting confes-sions from suspects. That uncertainty could logically be ex-pected to produce less effective law enforcement. It would lead either to excessively weak questioning, as police tried to be sure that any confession would remain admissible, or to the suppression of confessions when a court subsequently decided that police had crossed the invisible line into coercion.

The Supreme Court might have been able to develop more certain guidelines on a case-by-case basis. This would have been a difficult venture, for the voluntariness determina-tion is not easy to make on the basis of a paper record that might reveal very little of the tone and tenor of an investiga-tion. Even if it were possible, it would have taken many years and would have required the Supreme Court to devote a large part of its limited docket to voluntariness determinations. And even if it had produced a large enough body of case law to let lower courts make the determination reliably, police officers could hardly be expected to memorize all those decisions.

For all these reasons, substituting the bright-line *Miranda* rule for the voluntariness standard made good sense. It was certainly not compelled by the Constitution, but it was supported by plausible justifications. That meets the modest standard of legitimacy I have suggested. *Miranda*'s solution to the challenges of enforcing the self-incrimination clause may not have been the best one, but it is easy to see why it is reasonable.

LEGISLATIVE REACTION: *DICKERSON v. UNITED STATES*

If *Miranda* is only a reasonable solution, and not required by the Constitution, what happens if another branch of government thinks it has a better one? What if Congress proposes a different approach? In such a case, the Court should give respectful consideration to the alternative. If it seems likely to work as well as the *Miranda* warnings, then the Court should allow it.

In 1968, Congress did in fact respond to the *Miranda* decision by enacting a law that represented a different approach. What it proposed, however, was simply a return to the pre-*Miranda* regime under which courts considered the totality of the circumstances to determine whether a confession was voluntary. This law would have reintroduced all the problems that made *Miranda* necessary in the first place. The Solicitor General, who speaks for the United States before the Supreme Court, took the position that this statute was unconstitutional, and for many years the federal government did not try to enforce it. In 1999, however, the federal court of appeals in Virginia applied it to uphold the admission of a confession—even though the federal Department of Justice did not argue that it should be applied.

When this case, *Dickerson v. United States,* reached the Supreme Court, the Court was not faced with a situation in which Congress had carefully considered the reasons behind *Miranda* and offered a different solution responsive to the same concerns.[23] It was a situation in which Congress had simply pronounced that the Court's concerns were not substantial. In that kind of situation, there is no reason to allow Congress to override the Court's judgment, and the Court appropriately held that the statute was unconstitutional—a position the Solicitor General continued to maintain at all stages of the litigation.

Miranda and *Dickerson* show us a couple of important things about the creation of doctrine and the proper relationship between the branches of the federal government. *Miranda* shows that doctrine that gets cases "wrong" according to constitutional meaning, as by prohibiting the use of some confessions that are not compelled, may still make sense. *Dickerson* shows that when the Court's doctrine departs from constitutional meaning, there is a role for other branches of government to play. Their participation in the shaping of doctrine, however, must consist of something more than just rejecting what the Court has done. If Congress had crafted an adequate substitute for *Miranda,* the Court might well have upheld it. The same year as it decided *Dickerson,* in fact, it did uphold California's attempt to create a substitute for a procedure the Court had created to implement the Sixth Amendment's right to counsel.[24]

Executive Detention: *Hamdi* and *Rasul*

Following the terrorist attacks of September 11, 2001, Congress passed a resolution authorizing the use of military force against those responsible. Pursuant to this authority, President Bush sent troops to Afghanistan to topple the Taliban regime and pursue members of Al Qaeda. In Afghanistan, they arrested an American citizen named Yaser Hamdi, who had been turned over to American troops by Afghan allies.

The scope of anti-terror operations broadened, and United States forces began arresting foreign nationals around the world. Many of these people, who had initially been detained in places ranging from Pakistan to Bosnia to Gambia, ended up at the U.S. naval base in Guantanamo Bay, Cuba. In 2003, the Supreme Court heard cases brought by Hamdi, then held in a naval brig in Norfolk, and the Guantanamo detainees. All asserted that they had no involvement with terrorism or Al Qaeda and sought judicial review of the basis for their detentions.

The Supreme Court agreed with Hamdi, holding that he had the right to a hearing before some impartial decisionmaker, at which time he could challenge the facts that Executive officials claimed as a basis for his imprisonment.[25] *Rasul v. Bush,* the case brought by the Guantanamo detainees, presented a more complicated issue. The litigants in *Rasul* were foreigners held outside the United States. Apart from the question of whether these people were entitled to hearings on the factual basis for their detention, the Court had to confront the Executive's assertion that neither U.S. law nor the Constitution placed any constraints on how the Executive dealt with foreigners abroad.

The Court rejected this argument, though in a footnote and somewhat obliquely.[26] And it held that the statute on which Hamdi relied could also be used by the Guantanamo detainees to challenge the legality of their confinement. Its decision suggests that the foreigners held in Guantanamo are entitled to a day in court, though what rights they might assert remains unclear. The Executive, in litigation, has continued to argue that the *Rasul* detainees have no constitutional rights at all.[27] Congress, enacting a bill to consolidate and limit federal court review of detentions, remained agnostic; the Detainee Treatment Act of 2005 authorizes courts to decide whether the status of detainees has been determined by constitutionally sound methods "to the extent the Constitution and laws of the United States are applicable." That same bill, signed by the president on December 30, 2005, purports to limit federal court jurisdiction to the review of the decisions of military tribunals (convened to evaluate charges against detainees) and Combatant Status Review Tribunals (convened to decide whether detainees are "enemy combatants").[28] Detainees for whom no tribunal has been convened are thus apparently deprived of any judicial relief, a perplexing result.

Hamdi and *Rasul* sparked a mixed reaction. Those worried about the damage that the Guantanamo detentions were inflicting on the reputation of America abroad welcomed the *Rasul* Court's willingness to provide some oversight. Likewise, liberals concerned about the Bush administration's aggressive conception of Executive authority were reassured by the promise of judicial review.

Conservatives, on the other hand, tended to criticize the decisions, particularly *Rasul*. Attacks on *Hamdi* were made somewhat more difficult by the fact that conservative icon Antonin Scalia rejected the Executive's position even more force-fully than the majority did. The Executive, he claimed, must either prosecute Hamdi or release him; it could not hold him as, in essence, a prisoner of war.[29]

Mark Levin calls both *Hamdi* and *Rasul* "egregious examples of judicial activism," though he does not attempt to engage Justice Scalia's opinion.[30] His view of the two cases is essentially the same. Levin describes at great length the "thorough vetting process"[31] that the Executive has created to ensure that no innocent people have been detained at Guantanamo. Why, he asks, after the Executive has invested so much time and effort in making sure that these people are guilty—the worst of the worst, as Secretary of Defense Donald Rumsfeld put it—should judges get involved? Why are courts "more qualified or trustworthy to rule on detentions"?[32]

It is a good question. In fact, it is the key question. The issue in these cases is not whether the Executive has the power to detain those who are fighting an undeclared war against America. There is fairly broad agreement that it does, though matters become more complicated with respect to American citizens. And it is not whether the Executive has the power to detain without trial or charges loyal Americans or innocent citizens of allied countries. There is fairly broad agreement that it does not. (In court, the Executive has in fact argued that it can do whatever it wants to foreigners outside the United States, even if they are entirely innocent of wrongdoing.[33] But it has never taken that position as a public matter; its asserted authority to hold those it does, at Guantanamo and elsewhere, rests on the claim that they are wrongdoers.) The basic issue in *Hamdi*, and the ultimate issue in *Rasul*, is who will decide whether the detainees are wrongdoers or not.

Once again, this is an issue that can best be understood

by separating meaning from doctrine. The meaning of the Constitution is that the Executive may detain enemy combatants and not innocents. The doctrinal question is how to determine which category a given detainee falls into—or, more precisely, who will make this determination.

The Executive's answer, which Levin supports, is that this decision should be made by the Executive alone. Presumably it could be made by whatever procedures the Executive decides are appropriate, if judges are not to be involved. But in any case, it is to be made entirely within the Executive Branch. What this amounts to is an absolutely deferential doctrinal rule. Judges will never second-guess the Executive decision that a given individual is an enemy combatant.

To decide whether this makes sense as doctrine, we might start by looking at the factors discussed in chapter 2. Levin's argument, also made by Justice Clarence Thomas's dissent in *Hamdi*, relies on two of these factors. First, the Executive is better at making this determination. It will get the right answer more often than courts will. Second, an approach that allows for meaningful judicial review will be costly to enforce. Giving courts the information they need to evaluate the Executive decision will impose serious burdens on the counterterrorism effort.

It is far from entirely clear that these assertions are true. Whether a given individual has engaged in terrorism is the kind of factual question (who did what to whom?) that is the bread and butter of ordinary adjudication. Courts are quite competent to ascertain such facts. The burdens of disclosure are harder to evaluate, but courts do routinely receive classified information in sealed filings. It is certainly possible to imagine a procedure that would allow for meaningful judicial review without calling soldiers from the battlefield to testify.

The "thorough vetting procedures" already in place, which Levin seems to think are highly accurate, achieve that accuracy without any such intrusion into the conduct of military operations.

On the other side, there are basically two factors pointing in favor of a meaningful judicial role. One is the significance of the harm inflicted on an innocent person mistakenly detained. When a mistake by another branch of government will deprive an individual of something very important, courts tend to prefer rules that produce errors in favor of the individual, rather than against him. The other is the doubt as to whether the Executive can make the relevant determination objectively. Whatever greater competence Executive officials may have, there is cause to worry that their objectivity will be compromised if their superiors would like to hear a particular verdict.

With two factors suggesting greater deference and two suggesting lesser, this might seem to be a hard case, though also an unlikely one for the complete abdication of judicial review. But the generalization I offered earlier about there not being right answers to doctrinal questions turns out to have some exceptions. Some of the factors I mentioned—the two at work in this case—actually have the status of constitutional meaning.

The first principle—that judicial review should be less deferential when important interests are at stake—is essentially codified by the due process requirement that no person shall be deprived of liberty "without due process of law." What counts as due process will vary from case to case, depending on the significance of the interest and the cost and feasibility of different procedures, but the Due Process Clause does seem to tell us that people should not be locked up without an opportunity to present their side of the story to a neutral decision-maker.

Perhaps, though, that decision-maker can be located within the Executive Branch? Now enters the second concern, about the danger in allowing the Executive to be arresting officer, prosecutor, and judge all at once. Such an arrangement flies in the face of a very basic constitutional principle: the separation of powers. The framers divided government into three branches in order to divide it against itself. They hoped that by creating distinct centers of power they could prevent any one from threatening tyranny. The practical import of separation of powers is that significant deprivations of liberty cannot be achieved by one branch alone. To put a person in jail in the ordinary criminal case, for instance, the legislature must pass a law forbidding some conduct; then the Executive must bring a prosecution; then the judiciary must convict. Any one of the branches can free an individual, and no one by itself can imprison him.

The importance of separation of powers in protecting liberty is well established. In the 78th Federalist Paper, Alexander Hamilton wrote that "there is no liberty, if the power of judging be not separated from the legislative and executive powers." In Federalist 47, James Madison put the point more strongly still: the "accumulation of all powers, legislative, executive, and judiciary, in the same hands . . . may justly be pronounced the very definition of tyranny."

That accumulation is what the Executive has argued for. It claims the authority to go beyond congressional authorization, which extends only to actions against those responsible for the September 11 attacks, and to define as an enemy combatant anyone who has supported terrorism, even unknowingly and indirectly. (In court, government lawyers have argued that their definition includes "[a] little old lady in Switzerland who writes checks to what she thinks is a charity that helps orphans in Afghanistan but really is a front to finance al-Qaeda activities, a person who teaches English to the son of an al Qaeda member, and a journalist who knows the location of Osama Bin Laden but refuses to disclose it to protect her source.")[34] That changes the terms of the congressional authorization; it is legislating. It claims the authority to arrest and detain those it suspects of being enemy combatants, which is the Executive power. And it claims the authority to be the sole judge of whether such people are, in fact, enemy combatants.

Both the text of the Due Process Clause and the structure of the Constitution strongly suggest that, at the level of constitutional meaning, this is not permissible. The Executive Branch cannot wield unreviewable authority to define offenses and to determine whether individuals are guilty. The question here, remember, is not how searching or deferential the judicial review of the Executive's determination that a given individual is an enemy combatant should be. That is a question of doctrine, which *Hamdi* did not resolve, and it will have to be answered in later cases. What *Hamdi* and *Rasul* do is simply to reject the Executive's position that deference should be absolute—that there should be no review at all.

In rejecting the idea that Executive assertion is enough to support indefinite detention of American citizens, *Hamdi* clearly reaches the right result at the level of constitutional meaning. A vetting procedure that takes place entirely within the Executive Branch does no more to satisfy due process and separation of powers concerns than one in which prosecutors "vetted" suspects and then convicted them without the involvement of judge or lawyer. As the Court put it, "history and common sense teach us that an unchecked system of detention carries the potential to become a means for oppression and abuse."

What we have in *Hamdi*—and also in *Rasul,* assuming that there are some constitutional limits on what the U.S. government can do to innocent citizens of allied nations—is thus a situation in which the meaning of the Constitution forecloses one answer (absolute deference) that might have seemed possible as a doctrinal matter. (In fact, however, courts almost never grant absolute deference to other branches. When they do, it reflects a determination not that the other branch is superior at handling the matter—that is frequently the case, and it is no bar to deferential review—but that the Constitution prohibits judicial review, as when Article I Section 3 provides that the Senate shall "have the sole power" to try impeachments.) A range of doctrinal answers still remain available for the Court to choose from, for it has yet to specify the nature of the process a detainee is due.

This question is a difficult one. Reasonable people may disagree, and, given that the question is about doctrine rather than meaning, there is no single right answer. There are certainly reasons for courts to take a deferential stance, and the Court has historically been quite deferential to Executive claims of military necessity. To the extent that the relevant circumstances resemble the conduct of a war, deference appropriately increases. On the other hand, that deference led the Court into what is now considered one of its worst mistakes—the World War II decision *Korematsu v. United States,*[35] in which it allowed the race-based detention of loyal citizens on national security grounds. *Korematsu* was certainly on the Court's mind when it decided *Hamdi*—it appears in Justice Sandra Day O'Connor's opinion—and its object lesson may push the Court away from deference. What is clear—the reason that *Hamdi* and *Rasul* fall into the easy category—is that there must be *some* judicial involvement.

Further Reading

BROWN AND LOVING

Brown has generated a tremendous amount of scholarship. One classic study of the process leading to the decision, recently updated, is Richard Kluger's *Simple Justice* (Knopf, 2004). Another is Michael Klarman, *From Jim Crow to Civil Rights* (Oxford University Press, 2004). Klarman takes the view that *Brown*'s effect was actually relatively minor, an argument further developed and generalized in Gerald Rosenberg's *The Hollow Hope* (University of Chicago Press, 1993).

With respect to constitutional theory, a fascinating set of attempts to rewrite the decision has been collected by Jack Balkin in *What* Brown v. Board of Education *Should Have Said* (New York University Press, 2002). As I have noted, *Brown* has become a litmus test of sorts: anyone who argues that *Brown* was wrongly decided places herself outside the mainstream of constitutional thought and casts serious doubt on her methodology. In consequence, leading originalists tend to argue that originalism does lead to *Brown*. The most notable example is Michael McConnell, *Originalism and the Desegregation Decisions*, 81 Va. L. Rev. 947 (1995). For a more straightforward originalist argument along the lines I have presented in the text, see Charles Black, *The Lawfulness of the Segregation Decisions*, 69 Yale L. J. 421, 424 (1960).

MIRANDA AND DICKERSON

The academic literature contains many discussions of *Miranda* and *Dickerson*, a number of which take a similar view to mine. Mitchell Berman's article, cited in "Further Reading" to chapter 2, discusses both cases at length. Also valuable is Yale Kamisar,

Miranda *Thirty-five Years Later: A Close Look at the Majority and Dissenting Opinions in* Dickerson, 33 Ariz. St. L. J. 387 (2001).

HAMDI AND RASUL

In lumping *Hamdi* and *Rasul* together, I have essentially skipped over the question of whether the Constitution places any constraints on what the U.S. government can do to foreigners outside the United States. I largely skip it here because the Supreme Court seemed quite skeptical about the proposition that Guantanamo can be considered outside the United States for the purpose of determining the rights of its inhabitants. (As Justice David Souter put it at oral argument, the iguanas in Guantanamo are protected by U.S. law; can it really be that the people there are not?)

The issue of applying the Constitution beyond the borders of the United States is an important one, however. I have addressed this question in greater detail in a law review article, *Guantanamo and the Conflict of Laws:* Rasul *and Beyond,* 153 U. Pa. L. Rev. 2017 (2005). The argument there is lengthy and somewhat technical, but one aspect of it can be boiled down fairly readily. The federal government was created by the people of the United States to serve our purposes, and it has only those powers we gave it. I do not think we gave it the power to torture innocent people—even if they are foreigners, and even if the torture takes place outside the United States. Why would we? If we did not, then there are constitutional limits on what government officials can do. The precise contours of the limits are not necessarily clear, but the limits exist. And if they exist, the principle is established. The rest is simply the doctrinal matter of determining how the limits will be enforced—that is, the proper role of the judiciary in deciding who is an innocent and what sort of treatment they can be subjected to.

That article builds on the valuable work of Gerald Neuman, including his book *Strangers to the Constitution* (Princeton University Press, 1996). Other Guantanamo-related resources include David Cole, *Enemy Aliens* (New Press, 2003); Michael Ratner, *Guantanamo: What the World Should Know* (Chelsea Green Publishing, 2004); David Rose, *Guantanamo: The War on Human Rights* (New Press, 2004); and Erik Saar, *Inside the Wire: A Military Intelligence Soldier's Eyewitness Account of Life at Guantanamo* (Penguin, 2005).

III

Hard Cases

Chapter 4 discussed decisions that are clearly legitimate from the perspective I have developed. This is not to say that the doctrine they create directs outcomes that are always right in terms of constitutional meaning. The doctrine of *Brown* and *Loving* does—school segregation and bans on interracial marriage violate the meaning of the Equal Protection Clause—and likewise *Hamdi* and *Rasul:* due process demands some judicial involvement in the detention of Americans or citizens of friendly foreign countries. But *Miranda* and *Dickerson* will clearly and predictably generate results that are wrong when measured against the meaning of the Constitution: they tell judges to exclude some confessions that are in fact fully voluntary. They are legitimate nonetheless because it is easy to explain why their doctrinal tests make sense.

In this part, I turn to some cases where the explanation is not so easy. These cases are among the Court's most controversial—they deal with gay rights, abortion, campaign finance regulation, prayer in schools, the death penalty, and the taking of private property. They have inspired some of the fiercest attacks on the Court, and unlike the challenges to *Brown,* these attacks are ongoing. I believe these decisions can be justified, and I will explain why, but I do not argue that their results are compelled.

What that means is that a different doctrinal choice would also be legitimate. Overruling these cases would not go against the meaning of the Constitution. (Indeed, overruling *Miranda* would not go against the meaning of the Constitution.) Justices who have a different understanding of the significance of the various factors I discuss might legitimately conclude that a different doctrinal test would be preferable. These cases are up for grabs, and changing the Court's composition may well lead some of them to be overruled.

A nominee's assessment of the relative weights of these factors might provide useful information about which precedents she would be likely to consider wrongly decided, which is why questions about the factors might be useful in confirmation hearings, given that no one will discuss specific cases. Senators might ask, for instance, whether a nominee believes that legislatures are generally better than courts at resolving complex factual questions or balancing competing social values. Assuming that the answer to that is yes, a senator might then ask under what circumstances the nominee believes a less deferential stance is appropriate. What if the individuals burdened by a law are underrepresented in the legislature? If they are members of a racial minority? If they are poor? If history shows that the legislature seldom enacts laws for their benefit?

Those sorts of questions would be useful because they would tell us something valuable about a nominee's judicial philosophy—more than platitudes about approaching cases with an open mind, or being an umpire rather than a player. I find some answers more plausible than others, but I do not believe that many are clearly right or wrong. (Some judges I respect believe that identifying what I call "defects in democracy" is so subjective that it should be avoided entirely.) A judge's views on these questions could be called political, but they are "political" considerations removed to a level of generality at which they will not consistently favor any particular partisan side. They are formed not by narrow political preferences but by broader beliefs about the appropriate roles of judges and legislatures, their relative abilities to decide certain questions, and the relative dangers of too much or too little judicial supervision of majoritarian politics. They are, in short, the sorts of views that will affect how a judge acting in good faith will approach constitutional cases. They are views that the president, the Senate, and the American people should know about before giving someone a lifetime appointment to the Supreme Court.

Just as judges can reasonably differ about the relative significance of the factors determining the appropriate level of deference, they can reasonably differ about the best approach to cases where factors point in different directions. These are the hard cases. My aim in discussing them is not to show that the Supreme Court has found the only solution, or even the best one. It is simply to explain why these decisions are legitimate. By showing this—by identifying the factors that justify the Court's approach—I hope to focus discussion on those factors. The key issue in these cases is not constitutional meaning; it is doctrine. And if we hope to make progress in resolving these divisive issues, doctrine is what we should be discussing.

5

Gay Rights:
Romer, Lawrence, and *Goodridge*

The Supreme Court led by Chief Justice William Rehnquist was not generally welcoming to individual rights claims, and particularly not when compared with the Warren and Burger Courts which preceded it. But in one area this pattern was notably reversed. In 1986, in a case called *Bowers v. Hardwick,* the Burger Court upheld a criminal conviction under a Georgia law forbidding sodomy. The decision was a close one, five to four, but the majority opinion was dismissive and even scornful, calling the constitutional argument "at best, facetious."[1]

And then things changed. In 1996, in a surprising turn, gay litigants won in the Supreme Court, challenging an anti-gay amendment to the Colorado Constitution.[2] In 2003, in a decision that Court-watchers had long predicted, the Rehnquist Court overruled *Bowers* in *Lawrence v. Texas,* holding that gay sex could not be criminalized.[3] The *Lawrence* Court was careful to note that its decision did not affect the issue of same-sex marriage, but observers wondered if the logic could be so limited. And in the years following *Lawrence,* the Supreme Judicial Court of Massachusetts took the next step, striking down state family-law regime that limited marriage to opposite-sex couples.[4]

What are we to make of this course of events? Have judges taken sides in a culture war, as Justice Antonin Scalia and others have charged? More generally, what should judges do when they confront struggles over the proper place of particular groups in society? These are hard questions. But the model of doctrine and meaning that I have given will allow us to resolve them.

Romer v. Evans

In 1992, following the adoption by various cities and localities of ordinances prohibiting discrimination on the basis of sexual orientation in housing, employment, education, public accommodations, health and welfare services, and other transactions and activities, Coloradans amended their constitution by a statewide referendum. Amendment 2 provided that "neither the State of Colorado, through any of its branches or departments, nor any of its agencies, political subdivisions, municipalities or school districts, shall enact, adopt or enforce any statute, regulation, ordinance or policy whereby homosexual, lesbian or bisexual orientation, conduct, practices or relationships shall constitute or otherwise be the basis of or entitle any person or class of persons to have or claim any minority status, quota preferences, protected status or claim of discrimination."

How far-reaching this amendment was intended to be is unclear. We can distinguish several categories of people who might have been affected. First are private parties, who are generally allowed to discriminate, subject to limited exceptions.

Employers may generally refuse to hire, or decide to fire, people for fairly arbitrary reasons, with the exception that state and federal law in some circumstances forbid them from making hiring and firing decisions on the basis of race, sex, and religion, among other characteristics. Amendment 2 clearly allowed these private parties to fire or refuse to hire gays and lesbians on the basis of their sexual orientation—something they had been forbidden to do by the city and municipal ordinances.

The second category is places open to the public, such as hospitals, restaurants, and hotels. The owners and operators of such places are generally not allowed to discriminate arbitrarily; they have a general obligation to provide service to all who ask. When asked whether Amendment 2 would allow such people, whom the law calls "common carriers," to refuse service to gays and lesbians, the lawyer for Colorado suggested that it would. "A homosexual," he said, "would not have any claim of discrimination or special liability theory in a private setting after Amendment 2."[5]

The third category is the provision of government services. The government is generally required to offer services on a nondiscriminatory basis, by the Equal Protection Clause of the U.S. Constitution, if nothing else. But government resources are limited, and at times choices must be made as to who shall receive them. Though it is unclear, Amendment 2 might have meant that denying services to gays and lesbians was an acceptable method of allocating them in the face of scarcity. Thus, for instance, police officers deciding which complaints should have priority might have been able to put those of gays and lesbians at the bottom of the list.

This was unequal treatment, in two ways. First, by apparently altering the duties of common carriers and even government officials, it left gays and lesbians in a uniquely vulnerable position. Even with respect to private employers, Colorado law generally prohibited discrimination on the basis of any lawful off-duty activity, meaning that gays and lesbians were uniquely singled out in that context as well. Second, because it was placed in the state constitution, Amendment 2 required another amendment to undo. Gays and lesbians, uniquely, could not obtain protection from discrimination by persuading a city council or even the state legislature to include sexual orientation as a protected category; the political bar was set higher for them.

The Equal Protection Clause, I have said, forbids states from treating people differently based on hostility toward them, and also from imposing burdens on some group if the benefits that the law produces do not exceed the burdens. That is the constitutional meaning. In *Romer*, the Court found that Amendment 2 failed both aspects of the equal protection test. The disadvantages imposed on gays and lesbians were not related to any legitimate governmental interest; instead, the breadth and sweep of Amendment 2 made it "inexplicable by anything but animus."[6] In an opinion written by Justice Anthony Kennedy, the Court held Amendment 2 unconstitutional. "A bare desire to harm a politically unpopular group," Kennedy wrote, "cannot constitute a legitimate governmental interest."[7]

If one accepts Kennedy's description, *Romer* is not a surprising decision. Certainly, the Equal Protection Clause prohibits governmental attempts to inflict harm for its own sake. The debate over *Romer* is about whether that is a fair description of Amendment 2, or whether the justifications offered by the State of Colorado were in fact legitimate.

When pressed to come up with legitimate purposes that Amendment 2 served, Colorado's lawyer offered two. First, the

Amendment enhanced the freedom of association of private parties by allowing them to discriminate against gays and lesbians. Second, it expressed moral disapproval of homosexuality. These two justifications basically amount to the same thing: increasing the ability of private parties to discriminate against homosexuals (and no one else) is constitutionally acceptable only if the state has a justification for singling out homosexuals in that way. The only justification offered is the moral disapproval. So the question comes down to whether moral disapproval is enough to sustain the law.

In *Men in Black,* Mark Levin finds an easy answer in Justice Byron White's opinion in *Bowers*: "The law . . . is constantly based on notions of morality."[8] That is true, of course, and of course the fact that a law embodies a moral judgment does not make it unconstitutional. But most such laws, like prohibitions on murder and theft, have independent justifications: the activities they prohibit inflict tangible harm on other people. They are not justified in terms of moral disapproval alone.

For a better statement of the argument against *Romer,* we should turn to Justice Scalia. In rejecting moral disapproval by itself as a legitimate justification for the law, the majority came very close to suggesting that moral disapproval was indistinguishable from hostility. Justice Scalia, dissenting, made the suggestion explicit. Moral disapproval was indeed akin to hostility, he wrote, but "Coloradans are . . . *entitled* to be hostile toward homosexual conduct."[9]

In holding this hostility to be illegitimate, Scalia wrote, the majority "places the prestige of this institution behind the proposition that opposition to homosexuality is as reprehensible as racial or religious bias." That, he said, was a value judgment, a matter of "cultural debate." The Court's conclusion did not come from the Constitution, for "the Constitution of the United States says nothing about this subject."[10] Thus, it must have come from the justices themselves. And so in Justice Scalia's eyes, *Romer* was an activist decision: the Constitution left the matter "to be resolved by normal democratic means" and, by thwarting the democratic process, the Court had "take[n] sides in this culture war."[11]

This is a forceful argument, but ultimately it falls flat. The idea that value choices (or "culture wars") should generally be left to the democratic process has great appeal—but it is true only when the Constitution does not take a side. If the Constitution does, then the Court should do the same. So the appropriate question is whether the Constitution ever takes sides in culture wars—and if so, whether it takes a side in this one.

Does the Constitution take sides? Sometimes it does. There was a tremendous culture war over racial equality. Those who championed segregation and bans on interracial marriage were fighting to defend a traditional way of life and traditional values, and in the end those values were pronounced illegitimate. There was another culture war over the appropriate place of women in society. Here, too, the Constitution took a side, and what had been traditional values were deemed illegitimate. If Colorado had passed an amendment providing that blacks or women could be discriminated against with impunity, that would have been an obvious violation of the Equal Protection Clause. The Equal Protection Clause does not identify women or blacks as deserving special protection, but it is clear that a state cannot adopt a law intended to indicate disapproval of them, or to make it easier for private parties to discriminate against them. If a state cannot do that to blacks or women, why should it be able to do it to gays and lesbians?

But of course there is another question. As Justice Scalia

pointed out, there are plenty of laws that disfavor groups, and some of them do carry a message of moral disapproval. A culture war was fought over the consumption of alcohol, but the Constitution was neutral on that one until the prohibitionist victory was enshrined in the Eighteenth Amendment. And it is neutral now that the Twenty-first Amendment has repealed Prohibition. A state could surely prohibit the consumption of alcohol, even though that would impose a unique disadvantage on drinkers. It could also presumably take the lesser step of enacting something like Amendment 2—providing that some forms of discrimination against those who consumed alcohol were permissible. So there is the second question: if a state can do that to drinkers, why shouldn't it be able to do it to gays and lesbians?

At the level of constitutional meaning, there is no easy answer to this question. Blacks, women, homosexuals, and drinkers are all groups protected by the Equal Protection Clause, and if equal protection means anything, it must mean that they are all protected equally—none can be disadvantaged without an adequate justification.

At the level of doctrine, however, there are different questions to ask. The primary doctrinal question, I have said, is about the degree of deference that courts should give to the judgments of other governmental decision-makers. For equal protection, the question is how much courts trust those other decision-makers to weigh costs and benefits accurately, and not to impose burdens on a group unless doing so achieves real benefits.

There is an obvious difference here between blacks and women on the one hand and drinkers on the other. Drinkers are not underrepresented in legislatures. There is no history of discrimination against them, particularly not discrimination based on hostility or a belief that drinkers are inferior. Legislators who enact a ban on the consumption of alcohol will be affected just like everyone else, and there is little reason to think that they will not consider the costs and benefits of a ban with care and without bias. Moreover, if they make a mistake, there is no reason to think that they will not be able to perceive and correct it.

These things are not true of laws disadvantaging blacks and women. Legislatures that decide to treat blacks and women differently frequently contain very few blacks or women. There is a long history of discrimination against blacks and women, based on beliefs about traits or abilities that are now deemed false and on attitudes about appropriate social roles that are now deemed reprehensible. Last, legislators who vote to treat blacks and women differently will not (unless they are black or female themselves) be directly subject to the rules they have chosen. There is substantial reason to think that the legislators will err in their balancing of costs and benefits. And if they do make a mistake, the political power of blacks and women may be insufficient to prompt correction.

What these differences mean is that doctrine appropriately defers to legislatures with respect to decisions they make about whether to ban drinking, but not with respect to decisions about disadvantaging blacks and women. When laws that disadvantage blacks and women are at issue, the Court does not merely second-guess the legislature; it adopts doctrine that makes sure the discrimination will almost never survive.

Are gays and lesbians more like blacks and women, or more like drinkers? If you believe that homosexuality is a choice, and one which has basically the same appeal to most people, then it looks somewhat like drinking. But science does not support this view. On the other hand, openly gay legislators are few. And there is a history of discrimination against gays and lesbians.

That discrimination is based, at least in part, on beliefs that are now generally considered false—that homosexuality is a mental disease, for instance (a position once held by the American Psychiatric Association but abandoned in 1973), that gays and lesbians are more likely than straights to abuse children, or that "proselytization" can "convert" heterosexuals to homosexuality. In 1978, commenting on the Court's refusal to hear a case in which a state university refused to recognize a gay student group, Justice Rehnquist suggested that the question might be viewed as analogous to "whether those suffering from measles have a constitutional right, in violation of quarantine regulations, to associate together and with others who do not presently have measles, in order to urge repeal of a state law providing that measle sufferers be quarantined."[12] But the idea that homosexuality is a contagious disease is no longer widely accepted.

The discrimination is also based on moral beliefs that are not as widely shared as they used to be.[13] The percentage of adults expressing a belief that homosexual conduct is "always wrong" stood at 73 in 1973. By 2002, it had dropped to 55. Perhaps more striking, the opposition to homosexual conduct was concentrated among older respondents. In 2002, 68 percent of those over age sixty (down from 89 percent in 1973) believed homosexual conduct was always wrong. But only 48 percent of adults under forty-five (down from 56 percent in 1973) shared that view.

The situation that confronted the Court in *Romer* was discrimination against a group whose interests may not be well represented in the political process. That fact made a closer look at the state's justifications appropriate. The justifications turned out to be moral beliefs that are contested and apparently in decline at the national level, linked to factual beliefs that are now discredited.

This is the same situation that the Court faced with respect to blacks and women. The Equal Protection Clause did not end discrimination against those groups on its own, and neither did the Supreme Court. In 1873, five years after the ratification of the Fourteenth Amendment, the Court upheld the exclusion of women from the practice of law.[14] In 1896, in *Plessy v. Ferguson,* it upheld a Louisiana law that required railroad cars to be racially segregated.[15]

Those rulings were consistent with dominant national popular opinion, with society's understanding of the relevant facts and values (including, for instance, the sentiment that "the natural timidity and delicacy of the female evidently unfits her for many of the occupations of civil life"). Moral or religious beliefs that are sufficiently widespread may indeed count as adequate justification for a law, because if they are sufficiently widespread, they will seem natural reflections of the way things are, not controversial judgments. But society's views of relevant facts and values changed, and the Court followed. When the Court acted in *Brown,* and when it started striking down laws that excluded women from the business world, it was taking sides in a culture war. It took what it thought was the winning side, and history has proven it right.

History has proven the Court right in that the side it joined has prevailed. History has also proven it right in that people now generally agree that the Constitution takes the side the Court said it did—that the Constitution opposes those who would use the power of government to mark blacks and women as inferior or less worthy of respect. *Romer* represents the Court's prediction that discrimination on the basis of sexual orientation will eventually be viewed similarly.

The Court may be wrong. It does not have the power to bind society to its views, and if moral judgments shift back, *Romer* will not stand. But those who attack *Romer* as an activist decision are focusing their energies on the wrong target. The Court was not announcing its own moral judgment or seeking to shape that of society. It was reflecting an evolution in societal opinion. It was acting, as Chief Justice John Roberts put it at his confirmation hearings, as an umpire rather than a player. Whether discrimination against gays and lesbians is justified or not is a question that continues to be fought out in the arena of public opinion, and it will ultimately be answered by the American people. The Court has only told us which direction it thinks we're headed.

A number of factors make the *Romer* decision legitimate. History furnishes examples of discrimination against gays and lesbians that seem unjustified according to contemporary national standards, and the Court could plausibly have thought that state legislatures or even state-level popular majorities would not give adequate weight to the interests of gays and lesbians. But I do not claim that *Romer* is compelled. The Court could legitimately have gone the other way, on the grounds that the debate over the moral acceptability of homosexuality is still a live one, and that value choices should generally be left to the legislature. The Court tends to act, in situations like this, at the moment when it believes that it can predict which side of the struggle will ultimately prevail. So the timing of a decision like *Romer* or *Brown* is a judgment call. If the Court waits too long, it will produce a series of decisions that, like *Plessy,* end up looking shameful and insensitive. If it acts too soon, it will appear to be attempting to shape public opinion rather than reflecting it, and it may spark a backlash that will reverse the trend it believed was inevitable.

Romer did indeed inspire a backlash. Polling data show a sharp dip in public acceptance of homosexuality immediately after the Court's decision. But the trend toward greater acceptance resumed, and the Court has held to its path of reflecting this trend. The next step was *Lawrence v. Texas,* decided in June 2003.

Lawrence v. Texas

In *Lawrence,* the Court considered the constitutionality of a Texas law that criminalized "deviate sexual conduct," defined as oral- or anal-genital contact, between people of the same sex. (It did not criminalize such conduct between people of the opposite sex.) The Court struck down this prohibition as a violation of the Fourteenth Amendment's Due Process Clause, which provides that no state shall deprive any person of "life, liberty, or property . . . without due process of law."

How to get any sort of substantive content out of this language, which seems not to prohibit deprivations of liberty but only to require that the deprivation be accomplished according to proper procedures, is an important threshold question about constitutional meaning. I will discuss that question in greater detail below in the context of abortion. For now, assume the relatively modest claim that any law restricting liberty must have some adequate justification—basically, it must offer society benefits that exceed the costs of the deprivation of liberty. Assuming that, *Lawrence* posed two questions: what justification did Texas have for this law, and how critically would the Court review the judgment of the Texas legislature that the justification was adequate?

Both these questions had received a full-dress rehearsal in *Romer*, so the outcome of *Lawrence* was hardly surprising. The state interest boiled down to expressing its disapproval. Texas did not identify any tangible harm caused by the conduct it prohibited; instead, it sought to give legal force to a moral condemnation of homosexual conduct. As Justice Stephen Breyer said to Texas's lawyer during the oral argument, "You've not given a rational basis except to repeat the word morality."[16]

This justification might have been adequate if it were sufficiently widespread to seem a natural principle rather than a controversial moral judgment. And it might have been enough to satisfy an extremely deferential Court. But *Romer* had shown that neither of these conditions held. The Court was unwilling to accept moral disapproval of homosexuality as natural, and it was going to assess asserted justifications with some skepticism. Unsurprisingly, in *Lawrence* the Court concluded that imposing moral values on society through the criminal law was not a legitimate state interest adequate to justify the regulation of private consensual sexual conduct.

Justice Scalia, dissenting, argued with his customary verve that the Court had "signed on to the so-called homosexual agenda"[17] and had called into question all legislation based on moral judgment. Some commentators have read *Lawrence* to suggest a fundamental shift in the Court's approach to constitutional liberty, articulating a general principle that moral disapproval by itself is never an adequate justification for a criminal prohibition. That seems unlikely to me; I think the Court was clearly influenced by a sense that state legislatures were unlikely to weigh the costs and benefits of a ban on homosexual conduct accurately. I think it therefore reviewed Texas's asserted justifications more critically than it might in cases where there were no such reasons to doubt the competence or good faith of the legislature.

The question is important because much of the criticism of *Romer* and *Lawrence* does not focus on the laws struck down in those cases. There is no longer widespread support for the criminalization of homosexual conduct. At the time of *Lawrence,* some states had repealed their sodomy bans, and state courts in others had struck them down as violations of state constitutions. Only thirteen states still had sodomy bans, and those laws were rarely enforced. The ability of states to criminalize sodomy is not the real issue. What the critics of *Lawrence* and *Romer* tend to focus on is the possible future consequences of those decisions. *Lawrence* and *Romer,* they say, will lead to decisions protecting, among other things, masturbation, bigamy, adultery, incest, and bestiality.[18]

For some of these activities—incest, adultery, and bestiality—there is the easy response that a state wishing to criminalize them could identify harms independent of moral disapproval. Incest, even adult incest, is likely to present situations in which full consent may be suspect. Adultery harms a spouse and breaches the marriage contract. Bestiality can be considered cruelty to animals. For all of them, there is the further response that there is no obvious reason to doubt the ability of legislatures to assess costs and benefits, and that the social movements in their favor have not achieved nearly the success of the gay rights movement.

So there is little reason to fear that *Lawrence* foretells constitutional protection for those activities. But I've left one thing off the list, and it is probably the one that people are most concerned about: gay marriage.

Justice Kennedy's opinion in *Lawrence* states more or less explicitly that the decision carries no immediate implications for gay marriage. "It does not," he wrote, "involve whether the government must give formal recognition to any relationship that homosexual persons seek to enter."[19] Justice Scalia's dissent took issue with that assertion, too: "This case 'does not involve' the issue of homosexual marriage only if one entertains the belief that principle and logic have nothing to do with the decisions of this Court."[20]

The Supreme Judicial Court of Massachusetts seemed to agree with Justice Scalia. In 2003, in a decision that relied heavily on *Lawrence,* it held that the state constitution required Massachusetts to allow gays and lesbians to marry.[21]

Goodridge v. Department of Public Health

The Massachusetts court's reasoning in that decision, *Goodridge,* is quite simple. Marriage is an important civil right. The state may not interfere with individuals' ability to marry those they choose without some legitimate reason. And none of the state's proffered reasons is adequate.

Most of the interests that the state offered in support of the restriction of marriage to opposite-sex couples did not fit the facts very well. Massachusetts marriage law did not seek to promote them in any other way, and a ban on gay marriage would do little to advance them. The state argued that prohibiting same-sex marriage provided "a favorable setting for procreation,"[22] but Massachusetts law does not require married couples to have the intent or even the ability to have children. It argued that the ban helped to ensure that children would be raised by two opposite-sex parents, but the law does not prevent unmarried same-sex couples from adopting. The state argued that the ban conserved financial resources for the most needy, supposing that same-sex couples were less financially dependent on each other. But no evidence supported that supposition, and Massachusetts law does not make any attempt to limit the benefits of marriage to needy opposite-sex couples.

Last, the state argued that allowing same-sex marriage would "trivialize or destroy the institution of marriage as it historically has been fashioned." The court rejected this rationale too: "Recognizing the right of an individual to marry a person of the same sex will not diminish the value or dignity of opposite-sex marriage."[23] True, tradition reserves marriage to opposite-sex couples. But tradition likewise prohibited interracial marriages, and that tradition could not support a ban on interracial marriages once the supposed scientific basis for the ban was proved false. As it had with interracial marriage, the *Goodridge* court concluded, "history must yield to a more fully developed understanding of the invidious quality of the discrimination."[24]

The conclusion that there is no legitimate reason to deny same-sex couples the ability to marry makes *Goodridge* a direct successor to *Romer* and *Lawrence*, both of which relied on the assertion that the restrictions at issue served no legitimate purpose. The trend in these decisions is clear: courts will strike down laws that burden the interests of gays and lesbians until the state offers an interest that courts consider legitimate.

To predict what the Supreme Court would say about gay marriage and the federal constitution, then, we need to know what it would think of the justifications for restricting marriage to opposite-sex couples. Most of the justifications that the state offered in *Goodridge* would probably fare no better before the United States Supreme Court than they did before the Supreme Judicial Court of Massachusetts. The fit between the asserted goals and the means chosen is just not good enough unless the Court is being extremely deferential to the legislature. I have suggested that there are substantial reasons why the Court should not defer in that way, and *Romer* and *Lawrence* suggest that it will not.

One justification is somewhat different, however: that allowing gays and lesbians to marry threatens the institution of marriage. Justice Kennedy hinted at this concern when he suggested that the state could regulate to prevent "abuse of an institution the law protects,"[25] and Justice O'Connor's concurring opinion explicitly identified "preserving the traditional institution of marriage"[26] as a legitimate state interest. The *Lawrence* Court would probably have deferred to a legislative judgment that a ban on same-sex marriage served to protect the institution of marriage. Neither John Roberts nor Samuel Alito is likely to disagree. For the moment, then, the Supreme Court would probably reject a claim that the U.S. Constitution should be interpreted to protect gay marriage.

But only for the moment. Two possible trends might change its mind. First, increasing public acceptance of gays and lesbians might make the threat seem less substantial. Second, experience with gay marriage in the states might also suggest that it does not carry any harmful consequences for straight marriage.

In Massachusetts itself, the initial furor appears to have died down. An amendment that would have overruled *Goodridge* but allowed same-sex couples to form civil unions was approved by the legislature in March 2004. Massachusetts law required a second vote a year later, and in September 2005 the amendment was defeated by the decisive margin of 157 to 39. The reason, according to state senator Jarrett Barrios, was simple: a year later, people could see that their fears hadn't materialized. "We've got a world that hasn't changed."[27]

One very plausible way for the struggle over gay marriage to play out is this: As the years go by, other states join Massachusetts in recognizing a right to gay marriage under their own constitutions. The sky does not fall. Gay couples travel from states that recognize their marriages to those that do not. In these states, troubling cases arise dealing with parental rights and medical decision-making. Some states decide that they will recognize gay marriages from other states. Some, perhaps, amend their marriage codes to allow gay marriage. The sky still does not fall. Eventually, a majority of states, through legislation or judicial decision, have recognized a right to gay marriage. And then the U.S. Supreme Court does, too.

This process—a trend in the states that is then followed by the Supreme Court—is what happened with anti-sodomy laws and bans on interracial marriage. It is what happened with juvenile executions and the executions of the mentally retarded. And it suggests that opponents of gay marriage would do well to come up with some evidentiary support for the harms to traditional marriage. If they do not, a gradual process of acceptance by the general public will eventually be ratified by the Supreme Court. If it does this, the justices will not be imposing their own values on the nation. They will be recognizing a national consensus and bringing outliers into line with views that have become conventional. In so doing, they will be fulfilling the basic purpose of the Equal Protection Clause: allowing national values to override state discrimination in circumstances in which there is reason to doubt that the state-level political process will balance costs and benefits accurately.

Other possibilities do exist. Massachusetts may yet suffer some terrible consequences from allowing gay marriage. If that happens, other states will presumably learn from the experience, and the existence of a legitimate reason not to allow such marriages will become clear. It was just this process of learning from experience that Justice Brandeis referred to when he wrote that "a single courageous state" could "serve as a laboratory; and try novel social and economic experiments without risk to the rest of the country."[28]

Or the experiment could be shut down. In the wake of *Goodridge,* President Bush warned that the institution of marriage was being redefined by "activist judges" and announced his support for a federal constitutional amendment limiting marriage to opposite-sex couples.[29] The Federal Marriage Amendment has little chance of passing, which is a good thing. It is not needed to protect other states from Massachusetts. States have never been required to recognize marriages from other states if those marriages are contrary to their own public policy, so gay couples married in Massachusetts cannot demand that other states treat them as married. And it is not needed to protect the citizens of Massachusetts from their own judges; they can amend their constitution if they see fit. That, too, seems unlikely. The Massachusetts experiment will probably continue, and other states will have the chance to see what happens.

These paragraphs will sound odd to anyone reading this book ten or twenty years from now. They will sound odd because either they are so tentative about propositions that almost everyone in the future now agrees on, or they predict a strange future that never came to pass. In ten or twenty years, gay marriage will be either the personal computer or the flying car—it will be either something taken for granted in ways that were inconceivable to the past, or something the past thought would happen that now seems silly and unrealistic. (In ten or twenty years, of course, there may be flying cars. Adjust the reference if necessary.) We cannot be sure which, but my money is on the PC.

Further Reading

Bowers, Romer, and *Lawrence* have been the subject of many law review articles. Books on the subject include David A. J. Richards, *The Case for Gay Rights: From* Bowers *to* Lawrence *and Beyond* (University Press of Kansas, 2005); Andrew Sullivan, ed., *Same-Sex Marriage: Pro and Con* (Vintage, 2004); Lynn D. Wardle et al., eds., *Marriage and Same-Sex Unions: A Debate* (Praeger Publishers, 2003); Evan Wolfson, *Why Marriage Matters: America, Equality, and Gay People's Right to Marry* (Simon and Schuster, 2004).

6

Abortion:
Roe and *Casey*

I n 1973, the Supreme Court decided *Roe v. Wade,* holding
that the Constitution protected a woman's right to abortion.[1] *Roe* was widely denounced as a decision without a
constitutional basis, and it energized, if it did not create,
the national right-to-life movement. Overruling *Roe* became
one of the stated conservative aims, and a consistent plank in
the Republican Party platform.

A series of Republican Supreme Court appointees seemed
to provide the opportunity. By 1992, only one member of the
seven-justice *Roe* majority remained: Justice Blackmun, *Roe's*
author. The Court contained eight justices appointed by Republican presidents, and the only Democratic appointee, Justice Byron White, had dissented in *Roe.* The effect of the new
appointments became visible in a series of decisions chipping
away at the abortion right, and most observers believed that
when the question was squarely presented, the Court would
overrule *Roe.*

But in the 1992 decision of *Planned Parenthood v. Casey,*
an unlikely trio came together to save *Roe.*[2] Justices Sandra

Day O'Connor, Anthony Kennedy, and David Souter, Republican appointees all, wrote an opinion that reaffirmed *Roe*'s central holding. *Casey* changed *Roe* in some respects, but it continued to recognize a right to abortion. The Court, the joint
opinion announced, had called upon the contending sides to
heed a common mandate rooted in the Constitution.

One needn't remember *Casey* to know that the call for
consensus fell on deaf ears. Listening to pundits and senators
jousting over the recent nominations makes it easy to see that
the issue of abortion is still central to the appointment process.
Partisans of both sides view it as a litmus test, seeking clear
commitments through carefully phrased questions about the
right to privacy and the conditions under which the Court
should overturn its prior decisions. The nominees have carefully avoided committing themselves, but it is hard to believe
that they have not thought about the issue. They know what
they think. The rest of us can only wait to see what happens.

What should the Court do? In what follows, I will suggest
that both sides are right in some respects. *Roe* is a woefully unconvincing opinion, and *Casey,* though better, does not repair
Roe's defects. There is indeed something fundamentally wrong
with the approach to constitutional decision-making that *Roe*
embodies. All the same, there is a constitutional argument for
protecting a woman's right to choose. Paying attention to the
meaning of the Constitution and the way in which doctrine is
crafted from meaning will allow us to see both *Roe*'s defects
and the possibility of a different approach.

Roe v. Wade

The path to *Roe* begins with the Supreme Court's 1965 decision in *Griswold v. Connecticut*.[3] In that case, the Court struck

down a Connecticut law that prohibited the use of contraceptives. The Court's opinion relied on various provisions of the
Bill of Rights to find a "zone of privacy" protected from state
intrusion.

Griswold focused on the question of enforcement against
a married couple (though the actual litigants were a doctor
and the executive director of Planned Parenthood). And the
"privacy" it protected bore some resemblance to the ordinary
understanding of the word: it related to intimate activities
conducted out of public view. By "forbidding the use of contraceptives rather than regulating their manufacture or sale,"
the Court wrote, the state had chosen to achieve its goals in the
most intrusive way possible.[4] A statute whose enforcement required such prying into the private conduct of a married
couple could not be sustained. Read carefully, *Griswold* did not
announce a general right to contraception. If anything, it suggested that a law prohibiting the sale of contraceptives *would*
be acceptable: enforcement of that law would not have the
same destructive impact on the marital relationship.

The concept of privacy quickly changed form, however.
In the 1972 case of *Eisenstadt v. Baird,* the Court struck down
a Massachusetts ban on the sale of contraceptives. *Eisenstadt*
read *Griswold* to establish a right to contraception, and then
ruled that the right must extend to unmarried persons as well.
"If the right of privacy means anything," the Court wrote, "it is
the right of the individual, married or single, to be free from
unwarranted governmental intrusion into matters so fundamentally affecting a person as the decision whether to bear or
beget a child."[5]

Eisenstadt understood "privacy" to signify a right of au-
tonomy in making important decisions. The inclusion of the
reference to childbearing as a protected decision was entirely

gratuitous, but it clearly laid the groundwork for *Roe*. In *Roe*, the Court assumed that the Due Process Clause protected certain "fundamental rights" unmentioned in the Constitution. I will discuss that assumption in more detail later, but even granting it, a basic question remains. How should the Court decide whether abortion is one of those rights? The *Roe* opinion does not explain; instead it simply asserts that the right of privacy "is broad enough to encompass a woman's decision whether or not to terminate her pregnancy."[6]

Having found that the right exists, the Court went on to sketch out the circumstances in which the state might override it. After the end of the first trimester, the Court ruled, the state could regulate abortion in order to protect the health of the mother. After viability, the state could regulate and even ban abortion in order to protect the life of the fetus. This framework, the Court concluded, "is consistent with the relative weights of the respective interests involved."[7]

So it might be, but the legislatures that prohibited abortion evidently disagreed. The Court and the legislatures had reached different conclusions about whether the privacy interest outweighed the state interest in protecting fetal life. What *Roe* lacks is an explanation of why the Court has the authority to second-guess the legislative judgment.

The majority did not seem troubled by the lack. The tone of *Roe* suggests that deciding whether the legislature has balanced interests correctly is an uncontroversial aspect of the judicial role. But in a democracy, the choice between competing interests is generally left to the legislature. *Roe* is not a case like *Romer* or *Lawrence,* in which the law at issue is supported only by controversial moral sentiments. A fetus is a real being, and even if it is not granted the legal or moral status of a person, the state's interest in protecting it is fairly clear.

Roe's casual assumption of the ability to review the legislature's balancing of interests did not escape criticism. Justice William Rehnquist, dissenting, complained that the "conscious weighing of competing factors" was "far more appropriate to a legislative judgment than to a judicial one."[8] Even commentators who supported abortion rights as a political matter found the decision hard to defend. John Hart Ely, one of the greatest constitutional thinkers of the twentieth century and a pro-choice liberal, wrote of *Roe* that it "is not constitutional law and gives almost no sense of an obligation to try to be."[9]

As we have seen, *Brown* earned similar criticisms, but its place in our constitutional pantheon is now secure. *Brown* has moved from a bitterly contested decision to an almost unassailable one for two reasons. First, the issue in *Brown* is no longer a live one in American politics. In 1948, Strom Thurmond could run for president on a segregationist platform and carry four states; in 2002 Senate Majority Leader Trent Lott was forced to step down after saying that the country would have been better off if Thurmond had won. Second, *Brown* appears clearly right to modern eyes, for racial segregation employed to mark blacks as second-class citizens is an obvious affront to any reasonable understanding of equality.

Roe has benefited from neither of these developments. Abortion is still an intensely divisive subject, and the passage of time has not made the Court's reasoning any more persuasive. If anything, the developments in the Court's doctrine have made *Roe* appear less convincing. Absent some new justification for constitutional protection, the most that *Roe*'s supporters can hope for is that the new justices will decide that the time for reexamination is past. That was the message the Court sought to deliver in *Casey.*

Planned Parenthood v. Casey

Casey featured a challenge to a Pennsylvania law that imposed a number of restrictions, including a waiting period and a spousal notification requirement, on women seeking abortions. Many of these restrictions were fairly clearly inconsistent with the Court's earlier abortion decisions. The real issue in *Casey* was not whether the statute was consistent with *Roe*, but whether *Roe* would survive. Most observers thought that it would not.

Instead, however, Justices O'Connor, Kennedy, and Souter wrote an opinion that reaffirmed constitutional protection for abortion. *Casey* is a very long decision, stretching 55,000 words. In addition to the lead opinion by O'Connor, Kennedy, and Souter, it contains two concurrences, by Justices Harry Blackmun and John Paul Stevens, and two dissents, by Justice Antonin Scalia and Chief Justice Rehnquist. But at heart it is fairly simple.

The lead opinion contains two different arguments as to why *Roe* should not be overruled. The first suggests that *Roe* is actually correct: the Constitution protects a woman's right to choose abortion over childbirth. This right was cast in somewhat different terms in *Casey* than it had been in *Roe*. Perhaps in response to the objection that the Constitution says nothing about privacy, *Casey* spoke instead of liberty—a word that, unlike "privacy," can be found in the Due Process Clause of the Fourteenth Amendment. And where *Roe* had given substantial weight to the "right of the physician to administer medical treatment according to his professional judgment,"[10] *Casey* focused on the liberty of the woman. But the central point is the same. The liberty protected by the Due Process Clause, the lead opinion asserted, extends to "intimate and personal choices,"[11] of which abortion is one. The state may not place an "undue burden" in the path of a woman seeking an abortion before viability.

The second part of the opinion undertook an examination of *stare decisis,* the principle that the Court should generally not overrule its earlier decisions, setting out the circumstances under which such overruling was appropriate. Why this analysis was necessary if *Roe* was correct is not entirely clear. The lead opinion suggested that *stare decisis* somehow combined with the analysis of liberty, but again it is far from clear how this combination works.

The *stare decisis* section of the opinion identified four relevant questions. Has the rule of the earlier case proved unworkable? Has society come to rely on that rule, so that overruling it would impose special hardships? Has the law developed so as to undercut the basis of the earlier case? And have facts changed sufficiently to rob the earlier case of its justification?

The lead opinion found that the answers to all these questions supported *Roe.* Protecting a constitutional right to abortion is something judges can certainly do. Women have come to rely on an ability to control their reproductive lives, and that control has assisted their full participation in the nation's economy. The line of cases protecting intimate and personal choices had not been overruled. And while changes in technology have affected some of *Roe's* assumptions about when a fetus is viable, they did not affect its core principle.

Last, the lead opinion observed, *Roe* was a special case. It was the Court's attempt to resolve an "intensely divisive controversy,"[12] and in such cases the Court would undermine its legitimacy if it reversed itself merely because new justices had been appointed.

I will not say much about the *stare decisis* analysis. Justice Scalia, in his dissent, offered a point-by-point rebuttal, which is worth reading for its passion and eloquence, even if one is not persuaded by the argument. *Stare decisis* does provide a basis on which future Courts may refuse to overrule *Roe* (or, now, *Casey*), but there will certainly be disagreements over the proper application of the concept. If a majority of the Court comes to believe that *Casey*'s analysis of constitutionally protected liberty is illegitimate, *stare decisis* will probably not be a sufficient restraint. And so I will focus instead on that question. Is the decision that the Constitution protects abortion a legitimate one?

The Missing Justification

The way I have suggested we should analyze legitimacy is to start with constitutional meaning and ask whether the doctrine the Court has created is a sensible way of implementing that meaning. Our first question thus must be the meaning of the Due Process Clause, the constitutional provision from which *Roe* and *Casey* draw their notions of protected privacy and liberty.

One of the criticisms of *Roe*, I have noted, is that the Constitution simply does not mention privacy. It does, as the Court noted in *Griswold*, contain several provisions protecting the home—the Fourth Amendment restricts the ability of police to search a house, and the Third Amendment prohibits the government from quartering soldiers in a civilian's house under most circumstances. And one might, as *Griswold* did, conclude from this that government intrusions on the privacy of the home require special justification. But that sort of privacy is not the privacy at issue in *Roe*. Though you will frequently hear politicians talking about the right to privacy, that is a misleading label, and it will be much clearer if we take the step *Casey* did, and talk instead about liberty.

Choosing an abortion over childbirth is certainly a sort of liberty. Perhaps more to the point, compelling a woman to bear a child is plainly a severe intrusion on her liberty. But where is the constitutional protection for liberty? The Due Process Clause prohibits states from depriving people of liberty "without due process of law," but if a state legislature passes a law forbidding abortion it is hard to see what process is lacking.

The Court's answer here is that the Due Process Clause "has been understood to contain a substantive component."[13] It prevents states from enforcing certain kinds of laws no matter what kind of process they follow. To put it in more technical terms, the doctrine of "substantive due process" protects fundamental rights.

There are two problems with this sort of substantive due process. First, it is very troubling to anyone who believes in democracy. Substantive due process gives judges the authority to declare that certain rights are "fundamental" and protected against state interference, but the Court has never been able to agree on how to determine whether a given right is fundamental or not. Without any clear guidance on how to decide whether a particular right meets that standard, judges are more or less invited to use their own sense of justice. But American society is not supposed to be governed by the moral or political intuitions of judges.

The second problem with substantive due process is that it is not an accurate reading of constitutional meaning. This is not to say that the Due Process Clause does not impose any limits on what states may do. It does, and I will explain what

those limits are. But it does not do so by protecting fundamental rights. The idea that judges should be deciding cases
under the Due Process Clause by determining whether a right
is fundamental is bad policy and bad law.

What Does Due Process Do?

If you read any of the literature on the doctrine of substantive
due process, one of the first and most common things you will
encounter is the claim that the clause is only about process. It
is not about fundamental rights, and it can never justify a
court in striking down a law because of its substantive content
(what the law prohibits) rather than because of a lack of procedural safeguards. "Substantive due process," in short, is an
oxymoron—as empty of meaning as "green pastel redness," in
the words of John Hart Ely.[14]

The claim is in part correct. As I have already said, the
Due Process Clause does not protect some sets of rights that
are constitutionally special ("fundamental") in a way that only
judges can determine. That would be an odd provision to put
in a Constitution generally respectful of the democratic process, and it is not a natural reading of the constitutional text.
Nor is there any substantial evidence that the clause was understood that way at the time of its adoption.

But this does not mean that the clause is never a justification when judges strike down laws because of their content.
There is in fact a clear and natural reading of the text that leads
us to precisely that conclusion. The guarantee that no person
shall be deprived of liberty without due process of law means
that the government cannot restrict your liberty in even the
most trivial way unless it does so by means of a valid law.

What makes a law valid? The most obvious requirements

are procedural. Federal laws must be passed by both houses of Congress and signed by the president. State constitutions create similar procedures. But the requirements are not procedural alone. The federal government is a government of enumerated powers. The Constitution grants Congress a list of powers and permissible subjects of legislation, and it can exercise only those. If it goes beyond its enumerated powers, the law is invalid and courts will strike it down—as the Supreme Court has done in some important recent cases I will discuss in chapter 11.

This is precisely what the Due Process Clause (here the Due Process Clause of the Fifth Amendment, which applies to the federal government) tells the Court to do. An argument that the federal government has exceeded the power granted to it under the Constitution is in fact a due process argument—and a substantive due process one at that. Recently, it has been federalists and conservatives who make these arguments. They would be surprised to hear that they are relying on the Due Process Clause to set substantive limits on congressional legislation, but it is that clause that most clearly entitles an individual to judicial relief if the federal government goes beyond its enumerated powers. (The Tenth Amendment, sometimes considered an alternative, confirms that states retain those powers that the Constitution neither gives to the federal government nor prohibits the states from exercising. It does not, based on its words, give individuals any rights.)

What about state governments? They have broader powers than the federal government. In particular, state governments have the power to legislate in the public interest for the general welfare of the community—a power that Congress lacks. But, like the federal government, state governments derive their powers from the people, and if the people have not delegated them the power to pass a particular law, they cannot do it.

Are there any limits to what state legislatures can do in the name of the public interest? This is an important question that we will see again—in the next chapter, when I discuss the recent controversial Takings Clause decision *Kelo v. City of New London*, and in chapter 12, when I discuss the reviled decisions in *Dred Scott v. Sandford* and *Lochner v. New York*. For now it is enough to note that a faithful originalist should say the answer is yes. From the earliest days of the Republic, judges have suggested that there are laws that judges can identify as beyond the power of a state legislature. As Justice Samuel Chase explained in the 1798 case of *Calder v. Bull*, such things are not law at all: "An ACT of the Legislature (for I cannot call it a law) contrary to the great first principles of the social compact, cannot be considered a rightful exercise of legislative authority."[15] Thus, Chase's analysis relied not on affirmative rights but rather on absences of power. The Due Process Clause requires deprivations of liberty to be accomplished by valid *law*—an *act* is not enough.

But how are invalid laws—what Chase calls mere "acts"—to be identified? "The purposes for which men enter into society," Chase explained, "will determine the nature and terms of the social compact; and as they are the foundations of the legislative power, they will decide what are the proper objects of it. The nature and ends of legislative power will limit the exercise of it." There were some things, he reasoned, that the people forming a government would simply not want that government to do, and they would not delegate it the necessary power. "It is against all reason and justice," he wrote, "for a people to intrust a legislature with such powers; and, therefore, it cannot be presumed that they have done it."[16]

What sorts of acts might fall outside the scope of delegated power? Justice Chase gives examples: to punish citizens for innocent acts, to make a man a judge in his own case, to take property from A and give it to B. Most generally, governmental action is valid only if it serves a public purpose, or promotes the public good.

The idea that the government must act in the public interest is a reasonable one. The hard question here, as so often, is how to turn this general principle into doctrine that judges can apply. We can rephrase the requirement that a law be in the public interest as the requirement that it offer benefits that exceed its costs. (As we shall see, this is a somewhat watered-down version of the original principle, which demanded that laws make their benefits available to everyone rather than to some particular group. That understanding of public interest proved untenable, for reasons I will discuss in chapter 12.) So that is the relevant question in terms of constitutional meaning: does this law offer net benefits to society?

Having settled on the relevant constitutional meaning, our next task is to formulate doctrine to implement that meaning. The Supreme Court's early attempts ended up a notable failure. In those cases, which we will see in chapter 12, the Court took an aggressive stance and refused to defer to Congress and state legislatures. It struck down a series of laws that the elected branches of government thought were not just desirable but essential. This overreaching provoked an equally aggressive reaction: President Franklin Roosevelt proposed to add new justices to the Court in order to create a majority that saw things his way. This was the constitutional crisis of the New Deal, and eventually the Court backed down. It agreed that in the ordinary case, it would defer to any reasonable legislative judgment as to whether a law would promote the public good.

In most circumstances, this makes sense. Several of the factors discussed in chapter 2 suggest that the appropriate doctrinal test is a very deferential one. Legislatures are better at determining complex factual questions about a law's effects. They are also better at representing the interests at stake. Because legislators are elected by the people, their decision as to how to balance competing interests or values has a democratic element that judicial decisions lack. If legislators make a mistake, they can correct it, or the people can select new legislators who will.

But as chapter 2 pointed out, sometimes there will be reasons to doubt that the legislature will perform the cost-benefit balancing accurately or in good faith. Sometimes the burdens of a law will fall on groups whose interests legislatures might not understand, or might discount because the group is relatively weak politically. In those cases, the appropriate doctrinal rule is less deferential.

Is abortion such a case? Discrimination against women, the Supreme Court has said, is. Women are underrepresented in legislatures, and they have been subjected to a history of discriminatory treatment based on inaccurate stereotypes and narrow beliefs about their proper role. So one question we might ask is whether a law restricting abortion counts as discrimination against women.

The modern Supreme Court would say that it is not. Granted, only women can get pregnant, but not all women do. The line between people who are pregnant and people who are not pregnant, the Court believes, is not a line between women and men.[17]

That is true enough. But it should not end our analysis. The question is how well the legislature can be expected to represent the interests of pregnant people. All those people are women. The fact that the law burdens the interests of only a

subset of women does not make it more likely that the legislature will do a good job of balancing the interests at stake. If
anything, the fact that we are now dealing with a minority,
rather than all women (who are a majority of the voting population), makes it less likely.

If we focus the inquiry more narrowly on those who
actually seek abortions, the case for deference becomes even
weaker. These people are, of course, all women. They are also,
generally speaking, younger women. And, again speaking generally, they tend to be poor and unmarried.

So the question comes down to whether we trust legislatures to weigh appropriately the interests of young, poor, unmarried women. Stating the question that way might make it
seem trivial, but in fact it is not that easy. If abortion is really
a women's issue, we might expect to see solidarity among
women, in which case their majority status should be able to
protect them. (In fact, women support abortion rights in only
slightly higher numbers than do men, though younger people
of both sexes tend to be more supportive.) Even if not, we
might expect that legislators, aware that any law they enact will
affect their own wives and daughters, would have appropriate
incentives to weigh the interests accurately. And perhaps the
interests of men are at stake as well—carrying an unwanted
child is plainly a unique burden on a woman, but unwanted
fatherhood inflicts costs too. Last, if the concern is with whether
legislatures will weigh the interests of certain groups appropriately, there may be reasons to doubt them with respect to
young, poor, unmarried women, but surely similar questions
exist with respect to fetuses, who obviously neither vote nor sit
in legislatures.

The question is not easy, then. In the case of discrimination against women generally, I have said, one could legiti-

mately conclude either that courts should not defer to legislatures, or that they should. But the Court has said that deference is not appropriate in that context, and if that is the case, a nondeferential stance on abortion seems to follow inexorably. A minority group of women is weaker politically than women in general. Abortion restrictions line up with stereotypes about the appropriate role of women that the Court rejects in the sex discrimination cases. If even some of their support comes from such stereotypes, the political process is tainted. And the arguments that legislators will consider the effects on their wives and daughters, or on men generally, are not especially persuasive. Legislators tend to be well-off enough that their relatives could travel to pro-choice states or even leave the country to procure an abortion, and men have shown great willingness and ability to evade the costs of unwanted fatherhood.

So the argument for nondeferential review is fairly strong. If one accepts the Court's sex discrimination jurisprudence as a general matter, I think it is very strong. Even if not, the decision not to defer is a legitimate one: it is not a mere imposition of personal preferences. *Roe* and *Casey* are legitimate decisions.

That is not to say that they have settled on the best possible approach. Once we have decided that nondeferential review is appropriate, there is the further question of what form the review should take. Here, I will suggest, we can do better than *Roe* and *Casey*.

Fundamental Rights, Undue Burdens, and the Test of Sincerity

One thing that the Court could do would be to simply balance the interests itself. That is essentially the approach that *Roe* took. It seemed obviously illegitimate in *Roe* because the Court gave no reason why the balancing task could not be left with the legislature. But such reasons do exist, and to that extent the Court's decision to conduct the balancing itself can be justified.

Still, such an approach looks more like doing the legislature's job than reviewing its performance, and the modern Supreme Court tends to avoid it. Instead, its substantive due process cases focus on whether the asserted right is fundamental. This approach, I have suggested, is not a good one. It essentially ignores the key question of whether there are reasons to doubt the legislature's balancing. And it produces a stark dichotomy. Some rights are fundamental and can almost never be restricted, even for very good reasons—only "compelling" state interests suffice. Most are not; they are mere "liberty interests" and can be overridden for very weak reasons—any "legitimate" state interest is enough.

This approach is too rigid to work well as a method of enforcing the public interest requirement. It sets aside the legislature's resolution of conflicts between interests when there is no good reason to be suspicious, and it defers when such reasons do exist. Its tendency toward absolute deference or absolute rejection seems likely to produce a lot of errors—more, certainly, than an approach that focused on the reasons for and against deference and allowed for some intermediate method of review.

In the abortion context, in fact, the Court has moved away from the binary choice between fundamental rights and mere liberty interests. Though *Casey* claims to reaffirm the central holding of *Roe,* its "undue burden" standard is less demanding and more malleable than *Roe*'s test. Its applications are uncertain. Justice Kennedy, one of the authors of the lead *Casey* opinion, believes that it allows states to ban "partial birth" abortions; the other two authors, Justices O'Connor and

Souter, do not. (In *Stenberg v. Carhart*, the Court struck down Nebraska's partial birth ban by a vote of five to four, a result that Justice O'Connor's replacement by Justice Alito may change when the issue comes before the Court again.)[18]

Casey has created a space within which debate can continue, and, to the extent that *Roe* short-circuited the democratic process by which American society was resolving the clash of values, that may be a good thing. But simply arguing over what constitutes an undue burden is unlikely to bring a consensus solution that both sides can accept. The more likely outcome is that more conservative justices will chip away at *Roe* without explicitly overruling it, producing a regime under which abortion remains relatively available to the wealthy and well-connected but is increasingly inaccessible to the poor. That simply magnifies the current equality concerns.

A better approach would focus explicitly on the constitutional meaning at stake: whether the legislature has struck the right balance between the competing values of life and liberty. States should be able to decide, as a general matter, that life is more important than liberty. But they should not be able to decide that life is more important than young women's liberty alone. The issue, then, is whether the legislature has balanced accurately or whether it has impermissibly discounted the liberty interests of young women. (Or, to put it simply, if men could get pregnant, would the balancing come out differently?)

A court cannot decide this directly, but it could come reasonably close by investigating the way that the legislature has resolved other clashes between life and liberty, when the liberty at stake belongs to the general public. It could ask whether the legislature has imposed restrictions on the liberty of the public in order to promote life. Generally speaking, the

answer to this question is a resounding no. States do not require blood donations; they do not require people to make
their organs available after death. They do not, with few exceptions, impose a duty to rescue: a passerby can step over a
baby drowning in a puddle with no obligation even to lift it
out. (Parents typically do have a duty to rescue their children,
but they have no duty to sacrifice their bodies to do so—they
are not required to donate organs, bone marrow, or even
blood.) In these circumstances, it is hard to believe that the
state legislature values life so highly that a correct balancing
would force women to bear unwanted children in order to
protect the unborn.

This analysis suggests that, as things stand, abortion restrictions contain an impermissible discounting of the liberty
interests of young women. It also opens up a possibility for
states that do value life highly. By adopting life-promoting restrictions on the liberty of the general public, a state demonstrates and makes credible its commitment to life; it shows that
an abortion restriction might reflect a consistent and accurate
balancing. States could also demonstrate sincerity by taking
steps to minimize—and, more importantly, distribute—the
burden of unwanted pregnancies. They could offer substantial
assistance to pregnant women and mothers, thereby spreading
part of the cost to taxpayers. They could impose—and enforce—more significant child support obligations, spreading
part of the cost to the fathers. Distributing the costs of unwanted pregnancies more broadly would make it more likely
that the liberty interests of young women would be weighed
accurately, since the burden on them would be felt by others
as well.

States that adopted some or all of these measures would
have earned a greater degree of deference to their choices with

respect to abortion. How far that deference would extend is another question. It is hard to imagine another infringement of liberty as severe as pregnancy, childbirth, and motherhood. (Of course, many women actually enjoy at least the first and the last. Many women enjoy running marathons, too; that doesn't mean forced marathoning is not an infringement of liberty.) And if the state's interest in protecting fetal life increases with the duration of pregnancy, it must be weaker in the early stages. A ban even on very early abortions would strike a balance all but impossible to replicate in the general population. This approach might therefore leave an irreducible core of the abortion right intact in even the most determinedly pro-life state. But challenging states to accept widely distributed burdens in order to demonstrate a commitment to life would restore the life-liberty balancing to the democratic process.

Further Reading

The main text might be read to endorse the argument that no right to privacy exists because the Constitution does not include the word "privacy." On the contrary, I think this argument is fundamentally mistaken. The Ninth Amendment provides that "[t]he enumeration, in the Constitution, of certain rights, shall not be construed to deny or disparage others retained by the people." What the Ninth Amendment was designed to do was precisely to stop people from claiming that a right does not exist simply because it is not enumerated in the Constitution. Discussions of the Ninth Amendment may be found in Randy Barnett, *Restoring the Lost Constitution: The Presumption of Liberty* (Princeton University Press, 2004), and Calvin R. Massey, *Silent Rights: The Ninth Amendment and the Constitution's Unenumerated Rights* (Temple University Press, 1995).

To say that unenumerated rights exist, however, is not to say that courts should enforce them. I suspect that the original purpose of the Ninth Amendment was to give the public an argument to raise against the government, or rather to stop the government from justifying an oppressive law on the grounds that it violated no enumerated right. The Ninth Amendment, on this understanding, is a tool for the people to use to legitimize their resistance to the government. It is not necessarily a tool for courts to use. And since I can think of no good way for judges to decide what these unenumerated rights might be, leaving them to the people seems a sounder course. For a discussion of popular sovereignty with respect to constitutional interpretation, see Larry D. Kramer, *The People Themselves: Popular Constitutionalism and Judicial Review* (Oxford University Press, 2004).

In suggesting that the Court should abandon the idea that the Due Process Clause protects fundamental rights, I have neglected to mention one apparent cost of that decision. The original Constitution did not require states to observe such Bill of Rights guarantees as the First Amendment's protection of speech and religious exercise. The Court applied these rights to the states gradually after the Civil War. The reason it gave for doing so was that they are considered fundamental rights, and thus included within the Fourteenth Amendment's Due Process Clause. If the Court gave up on the idea that due process protects fundamental rights, it might seem to follow that states could restrict speech or religious exercise with impunity.

That is a complicated issue that cannot be addressed in this book. My short answer is that the Bill of Rights is more properly applied against the states through the Privileges or

Immunities Clause of the Fourteenth Amendment. There is a large scholarly literature on the subject; I would advise interested readers to start with Akhil Amar's *The Bill of Rights: Creation and Reconstruction* (Yale University Press, 1998). One might then argue that abortion is a privilege or immunity of United States citizenship. Unlike the Ninth Amendment, the Privileges or Immunities Clause is certainly intended for judicial enforcement. But I have no clear sense of how to determine whether abortion can be counted as a privilege or immunity, and so I do not attempt to make the argument.

There is of course an immense literature on the abortion controversy. Books I have found useful include Ronald Dworkin, *Life's Dominion: An Argument About Abortion, Euthanasia, and Individual Freedom* (Knopf, 1993); David J. Garrow, *Liberty and Sexuality: The Right to Privacy and the Making of* Roe v. Wade (Scribner, 1994); Patrick Lee, *Abortion and Unborn Human Life* (Catholic University Press, 1996); Kristin Luker, *Abortion and the Politics of Motherhood* (University of California Press, 1984); and Laurence Tribe, *Abortion: The Clash of Absolutes* (W. W. Norton, 1990).

The methodology I offer as a means for courts to ensure that legislatures are balancing values fairly was first proposed by Guido Calabresi, in *Antidiscrimination and Constitutional Accountability: What the Bork-Brennan Debate Ignores,* 105 Harv. L. Rev. 70 (1991). In suggesting that due process analysis should focus on equality considerations, I am not merely saying that abortion is really an equal protection question, as Ruth Bader Ginsburg argued in a law review article many years before she became a Supreme Court justice. The analysis I suggest differs from equal protection doctrine in two significant ways: first, it does not require an explicit classification by the legislature, and second it does not view laws that benefit politically weak minorities as equivalent to laws that burden such groups.

7
Takings:
Kelo v. City of New London

I n 2000, the city of New London, Connecticut, adopted a
development plan intended to create jobs and revitalize its
downtown and waterfront areas. The plan focused on
ninety acres of land in the Fort Trumbull area of the city,
some of which was privately owned. It proposed a comprehensive reconstruction including a waterfront hotel, a park
and river walk, restaurants and retail stores, new residences,
marinas, and office and research facilities. The plan was developed by the New London Development Corporation (NLDC),
a private nonprofit entity established to help the city promote
economic development. It was adopted after review by several
state agencies and approval by the state Office of Planning and
Management and by the city council. After approving the plan,
the city council authorized NLDC to purchase the privately
held land, or to acquire it by exercising the power of eminent
domain in the city's name.

Some of the private parties willingly sold their land. Others did not, and when NLDC informed them that it would take
the land under the city's eminent domain power, they sued to

stop it. The lead plaintiff, who gave the case its name, was Susette Kelo. She had lived in the Fort Trumbull area since 1997. Another plaintiff was Wilhelmina Dery, an eighty-seven-year-old who had lived in the same Fort Trumbull house her entire life.

The plaintiffs' argument was that the proposed development plan was not a proper use of the city's eminent domain power. Generally speaking, state and local governments have the power to seize private land for their own legitimate purposes. The takings clause of the Fifth Amendment places a constraint on this power by requiring that the government pay for land it takes. It provides that private property shall not "be taken for public use without just compensation." The dispute in *Kelo* was not about compensation, but rather whether the development plan counted as a "public use." The plaintiffs argued that it did not, because it was being implemented by a private developer, because some of the land would not be made available to the general public, and because some of the benefits the city predicted were purely economic: it would increase the tax base and create jobs. The plaintiffs lost in the Connecticut state courts and took their case to the federal Supreme Court.

The Supreme Court upheld the city's power to take the land, and a storm of criticism followed. The prospect of a city evicting people from their homes for these economic reasons raised public interest in the case. So did the fact that the plan was being executed by a private developer. And, surely, so did the heart-wrenching image of the aged Dery losing her lifelong home. *Kelo* was one of the most frequently mentioned topics in the Roberts confirmation hearings. Unsurprisingly, the senators could not get Roberts to venture an opinion on it, but several took the opportunity to express their own opposition—a worthy enough use of time given the impossibility of substantive discussion with the nominee. Senator Lindsey Graham of South Carolina did not even ask Roberts a question. Instead, he observed that he had "gotten more phone calls about the *Kelo* case than anything the Supreme Court has done lately." He went on to admonish Roberts that "the courts are able to do their job because the public defers to the court and respects the court, but there is a limit."[1]

There is something extraordinary about this statement, and something equally extraordinary about the reflexive denunciations of *Kelo* as judicial activism. The *Kelo* decision defers to a local policymaking body. It is not activist in any reasonable sense of the word. Graham was warning Roberts that there was a limit to what legislatures would allow courts . . . to let legislatures do.

That *Kelo* is not an activist decision does not, of course, mean that it is a legitimate one. Legitimacy is the more useful concept, and inquiring into *Kelo's* legitimacy will reveal some interesting insights. As always, we should start with the meaning of the relevant constitutional provisions.

Calling *Kelo* a takings clause case is in some ways a misnomer. The takings clause requires the government to pay just compensation for property it takes. But it does not, itself, either set a limit on the power of eminent domain or tell judges to enforce that limit. What does? The question should be familiar from the discussion of *Roe* and *Casey*, and the answer is the same. It is the Due Process Clause that protects individuals from governmental acts that go beyond the government's delegated power. Indeed, Justice O'Connor's dissent in *Kelo* opened with the same quote from Justice Chase's opinion in *Calder v. Bull* that I pointed to in the preceding chapter as the basis for substantive due process: an act that takes from A and gives to B simply is not a "law" at all.

Kelo, then, is really a substantive due process case. And if the restraint at issue comes from the Due Process Clause, the question we should be asking is the one Justice Chase asked: what is the limit on the power of eminent domain that people might reasonably be presumed to have given their government?

The answer to this is not that they would give the government the power to take land only for public "use"—in other words, only to make it available to the general public. It is easy to imagine socially desirable takings that do not fit this category. The government might take land in order to build public housing; or it might give the land to a private company such as a railroad, or a telephone or gas company, in order to make the company's services available to the broader community, even if the public was not allowed access to the property itself.

Indeed, it was just these sorts of takings that led courts in the early twentieth century to recognize that the public interest could be served by takings that were not for public "use" in the strictest sense. Both state courts, interpreting state constitutions, and the Supreme Court, interpreting the federal Constitution, consistently held that the only constraint on the eminent domain power was the one I articulated in the preceding chapter. As Chancellor James Kent wrote in his influential *Commentaries on American Law,* what the Constitution prohibits is takings that are "for a purpose not of a public nature."[2] The meaning of the Constitution is thus that takings must serve the public interest; they must offer benefits that exceed their burdens.

The next question is what doctrinal test the Court should adopt to enforce this constitutional limit. As I have noted repeatedly, the question of whether the benefits of a particular government act exceed its burdens is one that legislatures are generally better at answering. Moreover, their answers are subject to review and correction through democratic politics in a way that judicial decisions are not. Absent some reason to doubt that the legislature will balance costs and benefits appropriately, courts defer. As the Supreme Court put it in a 1954 case dealing with the federal power to take land in the District of Columbia, "when the legislature has spoken, the public interest has been declared in terms well-nigh conclusive. In such cases the legislature, not the judiciary, is the main guardian of the public needs to be served by social legislation."[3]

Did *Kelo* present reasons to doubt the ability of the legislature to balance accurately? The plaintiffs argued that the Court should review the public interest determination more closely when a taking created only economic benefits, or when the apparent purpose was simply to benefit another private party, or when the land taken was not destined for literal public use. Those reasons might be plausible, but they were not present in *Kelo*. The development plan offered substantial noneconomic benefits, including many literal public uses. It included a marina, a river walk, a Coast Guard museum, a state park, a hotel, and restaurants and retail establishments—all areas open to the general public, and all providing noneconomic benefits.

As for the private parties, Justice Kennedy's concurring opinion agreed that a "plausible accusation of impermissible favoritism" should trigger a more searching judicial review.[4] But that was in fact done. The trial court conducted a thorough review of the plan and the process by which it was adopted and concluded that the purpose of the development plan was not to benefit any identifiable private interests.

Last, both of the dissenting opinions, by Justice O'Connor and Justice Thomas, argued that the beneficiaries of takings for economic development "are likely to be those citizens with disproportionate influence and power in the political process"[5] while the costs "will fall disproportionately on poor communities."[6] Those are valid concerns. They suggest that the Court should generally defer less to legislation that burdens the interests of the poor, which is certainly a plausible claim. It is not, however, the approach the Court currently takes under the Due Process or Equal Protection Clause, and neither Justice O'Connor nor Justice Thomas has argued for it as a general matter. And once again, it was not the case in *Kelo* that the plaintiffs were poor.

Given the facts in *Kelo*, then, there was no substantial reason not to defer to the legislative assessment of the public interest. Despite the outraged reaction, the Court's decision was entirely unremarkable. It followed quite naturally from a line of cases extending back over a hundred years, and it makes good sense in terms of the appropriate allocation of decision-making authority between courts and representative government bodies.

And that is the ultimate doctrinal issue in *Kelo:* who should be making these decisions? It might well be possible to identify what Justice Kennedy called "a more narrowly drawn category of takings"[7] that should be subject to a greater degree of judicial second-guessing. But the idea that federal courts are generally the appropriate forum for debates over whether a taking is good policy, or whether it will achieve the benefits sought, is profoundly anti-democratic.

No one denies that the seizure of a person's home is a traumatic event, and no one denies that state legislatures or city councils may make mistakes in deciding whether the benefits of a taking exceed its burdens. Those kinds of errors are the risk of democracy. But democracy offers a remedy as well; legislators or council members can be voted out of office, and their decisions can be reversed by their replacements. Federal judges can be removed only by impeachment, and their decisions can be reversed only by constitutional amendment. The basic refrain of most of the Court's critics is that federal judges have assumed too much power and are usurping the policy-making authority of the representative branches of government. No one who thinks that should criticize *Kelo*.

Further Reading

The Court's takings jurisprudence is complicated and, until recently, has not been the subject of great public interest. The classic work on the topic is Richard Epstein, *Takings: Private Property and the Power of Eminent Domain* (Harvard University Press, 1989). Steven Greenhut gives the perspective of the *Kelo* critics in *Abuse of Power: How the Government Misuses Eminent Domain* (Seven Locks Press, 2004).

8

The Establishment Clause

One of the most controversial areas of the Court's doctrine—and perhaps its least successful, in terms of winning public compliance—has been the series of decisions striking down state-sponsored religious exercises or displays. In these cases, the Court has been enforcing the First Amendment's Establishment Clause, which prohibits Congress from making any law "respecting an establishment of religion." Establishment Clause jurisprudence is a vast and complicated field, which has presented the Court with many difficult problems. A comprehensive analysis would require a lengthy book, and it may well be that in the end no simple set of principles can explain all of the Court's decisions.

My goal here is considerably more modest. I will not try to defend each individual Establishment Clause decision. Some of them may be wrong—indeed, given the apparent inconsistencies in the decisions, it seems almost self-evident that some must be. But the critics of the Court's Establishment Clause doctrine mount a broader attack. The Supreme Court, Mark Levin charges, "has simply abolished your right to the free exercise of your religion in public."[1] It has done so, he suggests, in defiance of "the plain meaning of the religion clauses" and "because it wishes to dictate policy."[2] That is the attack I will address here, with the intent of showing that the Court's Establishment Clause decisions, though they may not be perfect, are a reasonable attempt to enforce requirements that have a clear constitutional basis.

The starting point for Levin's criticism is that the Establishment Clause was originally intended to apply to Congress, not the states. That is perfectly true. In fact, the point can be made more strongly. At the time of the ratification of the First Amendment, several states had established churches. The Establishment Clause was not intended to invalidate these arrangements. If anything, by depriving Congress of the power to make laws "respecting" an establishment of religion, it was intended to protect state establishments from federal interference.

So the Establishment Clause had a federalist dimension, protecting the decisions that states made with respect to religion. But it also had an individual rights dimension. It prevented Congress not only from dis-establishing state churches but also from establishing a national church. It did so in order to protect individual liberty of conscience, to ensure, in the words of James Madison, that Congress not "compel men to worship God in any manner contrary to their conscience."[3]

Still, that was a restriction on Congress and not the states. How did a right that individuals could assert against the federal government turn into one they could assert against states? Levin is not much help here. From his discussion of the founding era, he skips ahead to 1947, when the Supreme Court began to apply the Establishment Clause against the states. What this leaves out is the Civil War and the constitutional amendments ratified in its aftermath. The Reconstruction amendments, the "new birth of freedom" that Abraham Lincoln promised in the Gettysburg Address, changed the structure of the Constitution enormously.

In particular, they changed the relationship between the people, the states, and the federal government. In the framers' vision, threats to the liberty of the people were likely to come not from the states but from a more distant national government. That was the lesson of the Revolution, and the original Constitution reflected it. The pre–Civil War Constitution limited the power of the federal government. It placed very few limits on the states, and it sought to preserve their ability to check federal overreaching—by force of arms if necessary—through provisions like the Second Amendment, which protected state militias from federal interference.

The Civil War and Reconstruction taught a different lesson. The federal government had fought a war for liberty, and the defeated states continued to persecute their recently emancipated population. The threat of oppression, in the eyes of the drafters of the Reconstruction amendments, came from the states, and federal intervention was needed to secure individual liberty.

The Fourteenth Amendment does this in no uncertain terms. Its first sentence wipes out the Supreme Court's decision in *Dred Scott,* which had held that blacks could never attain federal citizenship. All persons born within the United States are American citizens, the Fourteenth Amendment proclaims.

With this citizenship come rights. "No state," the Fourteenth Amendment continues, "shall make or enforce any law which shall abridge the privileges or immunities of citizens of the United States." Thus, all federal citizens possess some rights that states cannot abridge.

What are these rights, these privileges and immunities? In the *Slaughterhouse Cases,* in 1873, the Supreme Court effectively nullified the Privileges or Immunities Clause by deciding that it protected those rights that federal citizens could *already* assert against the states.[4] Most academics agree that the *Slaughterhouse* reading of the Privileges or Immunities Clause is mistaken. There is far less agreement on what the correct reading is. In *The Bill of Rights: Creation and Reconstruction,* Yale law professor Akhil Amar conducts a careful study of the text and history of the Reconstruction amendments and concludes that the Privileges or Immunities Clause was intended and widely understood to protect at least the individual liberties guaranteed by the Bill of Rights. That is, to the extent that one of the first ten amendments protects an individual right, rather than a right of states, against the federal government, the Privileges or Immunities Clause extends the protection against the states.

Does the Establishment Clause protect an individual liberty? I have suggested that it does, even according to the original understanding. As another law professor, Noah Feldman, has argued in his book *Divided by God,* the Establishment Clause prohibited the federal government from establishing a religion not merely to prevent federal interference with established state religions, but also to protect individual liberty of conscience from federal infringement. Even if this is not correct, by the time the Privileges or Immunities Clause was drafted, the liberty of conscience understanding had emerged. And it was that understanding that the drafters and ratifiers of the Fourteenth Amendment would have thought was incorporated in the Privileges or Immunities Clause.

The Establishment Clause binds the states, then, through the Fourteenth Amendment. (The Supreme Court, declining to overrule the *Slaughterhouse Cases,* has reached this result by finding the Establishment Clause and other Bill of Rights freedoms contained within the Due Process Clause, rather than privileges or immunities. That is unfortunate—it is part of the reason that modern substantive due process jurisprudence has come to focus on fundamental rights—but the upshot is that what I am saying here is broadly consistent with what the Court has done.) The next question is what the Establishment Clause prohibits. What does liberty of conscience mean?

Here again, Noah Feldman offers valuable guidance. Tracing the idea back to seventeenth-century British philosopher John Locke, he explains that liberty of conscience protects the individual from compulsion in religious matters. In particular, it prevents the government from coercing individuals to engage in religious activity, or from forcing them, through taxes, to support religious institutions.[5]

Of course, these core principles leave open considerable room for disagreement about their applications to particular cases. In recent memory, no state has tried to establish an official religion, and none has coerced individuals, under threat of legal penalty, to profess faith or participate in religious activity. Instead, the Court's Establishment Clause cases have dealt with two main issues: religious activity conducted by the government, including in public schools, and government aid to religious institutions.

Of these two, the latter might seem the easier to handle. A plausible understanding of liberty of conscience suggests that the principle is violated any time the government takes money from taxpayers and uses it to support a religious institution or activity. Thus, a flat prohibition on the distribution of government funds to religious organizations might seem a clear and sensible way of enforcing the Establishment Clause.

This might have been true in the framers' days—many of the framers appear to have believed in such a principle. The problem is that the role of government has grown enormously. The government provides much more in the way of services and subsidies than it used to. To hold that taxpayer money may never be used to support religious institutions would now mean excluding them from a whole host of necessary public services. It would look not like impartial restraint but like discrimination against religion. In consequence, the Court has been moving toward a position under which the Establishment Clause is not violated by a government program that distributes benefits neutrally, to religious and nonreligious organizations alike.

There are still difficult problems that arise with this approach. What, for instance, should the Court do if a state decides to make funds available to organizations performing a certain function, and most of those happen to be religious? That was essentially the issue presented by the Cleveland school voucher program the Court considered in the 2000 case of *Zelman v. Simmons-Harris*.[6] The voucher program made funds available for public school students to attend private school if they chose. Eighty-two percent of the participating schools had a religious affiliation, and 96 percent of the students who used vouchers ended up in religious schools—sometimes despite the fact that their parents would have preferred an equally good nonreligious school.

In that case, government funds were going overwhelmingly to religious institutions, where they were used in part for religious instruction. The Supreme Court nonetheless upheld the voucher program against an Establishment Clause challenge. The fact that parents exercised choice in selecting schools, the Court said, meant that the program did not amount to a government attempt to promote religion. That was so even though it was clear that religious organizations would receive the lion's share of the benefits no matter what the parents wanted, simply because the vast majority of participating schools were religious. *Zelman* is not the work of a Court that is determinedly hostile to religion.

In the area of state religious exercise, the picture is murkier. Here, the Court has confronted two basic types of activity: religious displays, and prayer in schools. The focus of cases dealing with the former has been whether the display conveys a message of state endorsement of religion. In cases dealing with the latter, the Court has asked whether individuals will feel coerced into participation.

These are reasonable questions to focus on in terms of constitutional meaning. When the state erects a religious display, it uses taxpayer funds to promote a religion that not all taxpayers support or want to be associated with. That violates one of the principles of liberty of conscience. It also sends a message that one religion is preferred over others. That is not consistent even with the idea that what the Establishment Clause requires is neutrality among religions. (A sufficiently inclusive, nonsectarian display might attain neutrality, but the increasing religious diversity of America has made this much more difficult than it used to be.) And if the state conducts religious exercises in such a manner that individuals feel pressure to participate, it has induced them to profess a faith they do not hold—a violation of the core of the liberty of conscience principle.

In terms of meaning, then, the things the Court is trying to prevent—government preferences for particular religions, and coerced participation in religious exercise—are plausible violations of a reasonable understanding of the Establishment Clause. Most religious believers probably do not quarrel with these principles. They do not seek to harness the power of the state to proclaim that theirs is the one true faith, and they would not think of forcing others to join them in religious ceremonies. The discontent with the Court's decisions stems more from the fact that the doctrine the Court has developed to implement this understanding of constitutional meaning is not deferential but rather fairly aggressive. It is highly sensitive to the possibility of coercion, and it is broad in its understanding of what counts as a prohibited endorsement.

There are substantial reasons that support this aggressive stance. The democratic process cannot necessarily be relied on, for majorities are not always willing to accommodate the sensibilities of religious minorities. If they were, there would be no need for the Establishment Clause, or the adjacent First Amendment provision protecting the free exercise of religion. And even when majorities act with the best intentions, it may be hard for them to perceive coercion or endorsement in their own familiar religious symbols and activities. Familiar things seem innocent to those familiar with them.

Additionally, history shows that the public has resisted the Supreme Court's rulings. They may do so for good reasons—they may do so because they can see that the Court's doctrine prohibits government acts that do not, in fact, violate constitutional meaning—but they have demonstrated an unwillingness to follow the rules the Court has set out. This adversarial stance on the part of state and local officials has understandably made the Court less ready to trust their good faith. In 1985, for instance, the Court struck down an Alabama law requiring a one-minute period of silence in public schools "for meditation or voluntary prayer."[7] It did so not because there is anything wrong with schoolchildren praying voluntarily, but because the Court concluded that the sole purpose of the law was to express state approval of prayer—that is, it was an attempt to get around the Court's decision that state-sponsored prayers could not be conducted in public school. Popular resistance may also explain why the Court has chosen to mold its doctrine in the form of standards, rather than manipulable rules.

The Court's decisions, then, are legitimate as I use the term. They follow plausibly from a plausible understanding of constitutional meaning. The Court has not embarked on an anti-religious crusade, and it has certainly not abolished your right to free exercise of religion in public. The Court has consistently held that private religious displays, and private religious speech, are allowed in the public arena on equal terms with other kinds of speech. Indeed, they cannot be shut out. If the government opens up a public square for expressive activities, it must allow a private group to erect crosses there.[8] If a university funds student publications, it must fund a religious paper offering "a Christian perspective."[9] And if a school makes facilities available to student groups, it cannot exclude groups that wish to use them "for purposes of religious worship and teaching."[10]

But again, to say that the Court's decisions are legitimate is not to say that they are the best approach. Another consideration in crafting doctrine is the cost of error. Here the Court seems to have underestimated the cost it imposes on religious believers when it excludes religious expression from the public sphere. The government now presides over many significant events, such as public high school graduations, which believers wish to solemnize with religious ceremonies. Prohibiting essentially all official prayer at public school events because of the danger of coercion might be striking the wrong balance.

Perhaps more seriously, the doctrine is on the verge of running into official practices the Court is clearly unwilling to prohibit. A straightforward application of the endorsement test might well find unconstitutional things such as the recitation of the Pledge of Allegiance (with its reference to a nation "under God") in public schools, or the display of the phrase "In God We Trust" on U.S. currency. The Supreme Court is not about to strike down either of those. It would prefer to avoid the question. When a federal appeals court held recitation of the pledge unconstitutional in 2003, the Supreme Court managed to undo that decision on technical grounds.[11] If the issue is forced upon it again, the Court will probably find that the pledge and the currency are patriotic, rather than religious, in nature. But it might do better to adopt a less demanding doctrinal test.

The Establishment Clause presents the Court with some very difficult questions. The Court has addressed those questions in good faith and to the best of its ability; there are sensible justifications for the rules it has come up with. But the creation of doctrine is an ongoing task, and in the future the Court may well shift its approach to the Establishment Clause. There are other legitimate choices out there. Some may be preferable to the existing doctrine, and the additions of Justice Alito and Chief Justice Roberts may lead the Court to them. It is this process—the appointment of justices who have a different assessment of the relative significance of various factors in the creation of doctrine—that allows the president and the senators, representing the people, to influence doctrine. As citizens, we should look to that process to change doctrine we feel is mistaken. Legitimate doctrinal choices are not a reason to condemn the Court.

Further Reading

My account of the origins and evolution of the Establishment Clause relies, as the text notes, on Akhil Amar, *The Bill of Rights: Creation and Reconstruction* (Yale University Press, 1998), and Noah Feldman, *Divided by God* (Farrar, Straus and Giroux, 2005). Other useful studies include Thomas J. Curry, *The First Freedoms: Church and State in America to the Passage of the First Amendment* (Oxford University Press, 1985); Philip A. Hamburger, *Separation of Church and State* (Harvard University Press, 2002); William R. Hutchison, *Religious Pluralism in America: The Contentious History of a Founding Ideal* (Yale University Press, 2003); Mark DeWolfe Howe, *The Garden and the Wilderness: Religion and Government in American Constitutional History* (University of Chicago Press, 1965); Leonard W. Levy, *The Establishment Clause* (University of North Carolina Press, 1994); William Lee Miller, *The First Liberty: Religion and the American Republic* (Knopf, 1986); and Steven D. Smith, *Foreordained Failure: The Quest for a Constitutional Principle of Religious Freedom* (Oxford University Press, 1995).

9

The Death Penalty:
Roper and *Atkins*

I n two recent decisions, the Supreme Court has restricted
the ability of states to execute criminals. In 2002, in *Atkins
v. Virginia,*[1] it held that the Cruel and Unusual Punishment
Clause of the Eighth Amendment prohibited the imposition of the death penalty on mentally retarded offenders. And
in 2005, in *Roper v. Simmons,*[2] it held that the same clause prohibited the execution of criminals who were under eighteen
years old when they committed their crimes.

Public reaction to these decisions, *Roper* in particular,
was quite negative, even among liberals. Writing in *The New
Republic,* Jeffrey Rosen described an "unusually scathing" reaction in the Supreme Court pressroom, and a consensus among
the ideologically diverse journalists gathered there that "*Roper
v. Simmons* is indeed embarrassing."[3]

Why should this be so? Critics have focused on two components of *Roper* and *Atkins*. The first is the idea that the
Eighth Amendment can prohibit today practices that it allowed twenty or a hundred years ago. The second is the idea

that the practices and laws of foreign countries might have some relevance to the question of what the amendment forbids. Considering how meaning relates to doctrine will help us understand whether the criticism is well founded. *Atkins,* I will suggest, is relatively unproblematic. *Roper* is more troubling, though the problem there has less to do with the consideration of foreign law than with the Court's understanding of the Eighth Amendment.

A preliminary question about meaning is whether the Eighth Amendment is better understood as fixed or flexible in its applications. I have argued already (in chapter 2) that the meaning of a constitutional provision can remain constant while its applications change. A flexible range of applications is not inconsistent with originalism. The only question is whether the Eighth Amendment was originally understood to prohibit a fixed set of punishments—those deemed "cruel and unusual" at the time of its ratification—or whether it was understood to prohibit punishments with certain characteristics, with the understanding that punishments that were not considered cruel and unusual when the Eighth Amendment was ratified might become so.

As far as the plain language of the Constitution goes, both "cruel" and "unusual" are more plausibly read as referring to evolving attitudes and practices than to those of 1791. The clause's own historical origins, as ably recounted by Justice Antonin Scalia in the 1991 decision of *Harmelin v. Michigan,* support this reading.[4] It does seem clear that the antecedent of the Cruel and Unusual Punishment Clause was a similar provision in the English Declaration of Rights of 1689. But "unusual" there meant contrary to the common law. This meaning could not be transferred to the context of America, where common law punishments did not exist. "Unusual" therefore presumably means rare—in the words of Justice Scalia, "not regularly or customarily employed."[5]

What about "cruel"? It seems unlikely that the framers intended to prohibit only a set of practices that they, or the English of 1689, recognized as cruel. (The English Bill of Rights, in fact, objected not to particular modes of punishment but to their discretionary imposition by judges.) A provision targeting particular practices could simply have listed them. If the intent was instead to prohibit as a general matter practices that society considered barbaric or inhumane, the logic behind the prohibition—that barbarism is bad—is better served by an interpretation that applies contemporary understandings of cruelty. A fixed set of applications will inevitably lead either to tolerating barbarism or to prohibiting sensible punishments, depending on the direction of societal change—and reasonable readers of the Eighth Amendment would have understood this.

The real dispute over the meaning of "cruel" is more about whether it relates only to the mode of punishment, or whether it includes a proportionality component—whether, that is, a punishment can be "cruel" with respect to one crime (say, shoplifting) but not with respect to another (say, murder). In *Harmelin*, Justice Scalia argued against a proportionality component to the concept of cruelty. But the English legal sources he cites suggest that this aspect did exist. The Declaration of Rights of 1689 objected to punishments imposed by the notorious Lord Chief Justice Jeffreys, calling them cruel. That evaluation could not have been meant in the abstract, since such punishments—drawing and quartering, beheading, burning, and disemboweling—were at the time both common and authorized by law. What made them cruel must have been the fact that they were not warranted by the offenses committed.

As the dissenters to one of Jeffreys's rulings protested, "said Judgments are barbarous, inhuman, and unchristian; and there is no Precedent to warrant the Punishments of whipping and committing to Prison for Life, for the Crime of Perjury."[6]

The idea that proportionality has a place in Eighth Amendment analysis is not a newcomer to American constitutional law. The Supreme Court endorsed it as early as 1910, in a case called *Weems v. United States*.[7] By the time of *Harmelin*, the Court had regularly applied it in evaluating death sentences, holding, for instance, that death could not be imposed for rape of an adult, or for murders committed by an accomplice where the defendant himself lacked the intent to kill. In *Harmelin*, in fact, Justice Scalia accepted that proportionality played a role in the context of the death penalty, commenting only that he "would leave it there" and not apply it more generally.[8]

So the meaning of the Eighth Amendment—or at least a plausible and widely accepted version of that meaning—is that it prohibits punishments that are rarely used because many or most people consider them too harsh for a given crime. On this understanding, the Eighth Amendment now prohibits some things that it used to allow. That is not very controversial. Nor is it controversial that the Amendment prohibits the imposition of the death sentence for some crimes. The judgment that *Roper* and *Atkins* reflect is that juveniles and the mentally retarded are not as blameworthy as fully competent adults, and that therefore execution is too severe a punishment. If this judgment has been accepted widely enough to constitute a national consensus, imposing the death penalty on such people will be cruel and unusual, and the Eighth Amendment will prohibit it. The dispute over *Atkins* and *Roper* is, as is so often the case, not so much about this constitutional

meaning as about the approach the Court has taken in deciding whether a sufficient consensus exists. That is, it is about
doctrine.

How should the Court go about deciding what constitutes a sufficient consensus? When the Court held that death
was a disproportionate punishment for rape of an adult, the
imbalance was overwhelming: only one state authorized such
a penalty. In *Atkins* and *Roper,* the evidence was considerably
less powerful. Twelve states did not impose the death penalty
at all. Of the thirty-eight that did, eighteen (and the federal
government) exempted juveniles and the mentally retarded.

Is that enough? It is important to remember that the
distinction between doctrine and meaning makes this two
different questions. The first, at the level of meaning, asks
what is enough of a consensus for a punishment to be cruel
and unusual. The second, at the level of doctrine, asks what
the Court should require before pronouncing that such a
consensus exists.

The distinction is subtle, but it is real. It is significant because, as I have argued repeatedly, the doctrinal test may diverge from constitutional meaning. Suppose, for instance, that
the Court's view of constitutional meaning is that a practice
should be considered cruel and unusual if two-thirds of the national population disapproves. Such a Court might look to
opinion polls, or it might decide that legislation provides better evidence of actual considered judgment. And having decided to look to state legislation, the Court might further adopt
a doctrinal test demanding evidence of a greater—or a lesser—
consensus than it believed constitutional meaning required.

Why would doctrine diverge from meaning? Again, various factors can be offered in support of more or less demanding doctrinal tests. The more demanding test is somewhat

harder to explain. The chief supporting factor is probably the cost of error. The point is that it is much easier to change laws than to reverse constitutional decisions. If the Court fails to recognize a consensus that exists, it can always do so later. If it finds consensus where none exists, it has taken the issue away from the democratic process in a manner unlikely to be remedied. Thus, justices highly concerned with the value of democratic self-governance might demand evidence of a very substantial consensus—more than the Constitution itself requires—before they were willing to hold a punishment unconstitutional.

Factors also exist on the other side. In *Atkins,* the Court alluded to "the well-known fact that anticrime legislation is far more popular than legislation providing protections for persons guilty of violent crime."[9] Politicians afraid of being labeled soft on crime might hesitate to support legislation prohibiting certain punishments, and the pattern of state legislative practices might therefore underrepresent societal disapproval of that punishment. Thus, the Court might decide for the purposes of doctrine to accept a "consensus" of less than two-thirds of the states. It might also think that the cost of error factor pointed the other way—that the cost of erroneously allowing the death penalty in cases in which society has rejected it vastly exceeds the cost of prohibiting it in cases in which society accepts it. This would be especially true if the Court's mistake amounted only to jumping the gun—holding that a consensus existed where it did not, but would have in a few years.

With factors on both sides, it is legitimate for the Court either to act aggressively or to defer. The majorities in *Roper* and *Atkins* are aggressive. What motivates them, I suspect, is a belief that they have identified a trend that would continue in the absence of judicial intervention. In other words, had the Court not ruled the way it did, the majorities in both cases believed that a consensus *would* emerge in the relatively near future, even if it did not exist at the time of their decisions. If that is true, the cost of prohibiting some executions that society would soon deem unjustified is fairly slight, especially given the terrible irrevocability of the death penalty.

The Relevance of Foreign Law

That explains, at least partially, the outcome in *Atkins* and *Roper*. The evidence of actual consensus may be slim, but the justices believe the evidence suggests that a consensus is emerging. But what about the reliance on foreign laws and practices? This is probably the most controversial aspect of the decisions. It is what Jeffrey Rosen calls an "invitation to the worst kind of judicial activism," and it has inspired bills prohibiting federal courts from considering such materials.[10] (These bills are unlikely to become law, and their constitutionality is doubtful, but they certainly indicate opposition to the practice.)

The answer here is somewhat complicated. It will be useful to distinguish three different ways in which the decisions might "rely" on foreign law. First, they might be using foreign law to decide whether imposing the death penalty on juveniles or the mentally retarded is unusual. Second, they might use it to decide whether the punishment is cruel. And last, they might use it to help decide whether an apparent American consensus was likely to prove stable or not.

The first option amounts to counting not just American states and the federal government, but also foreign countries in deciding whether a majority has rejected certain punishments. That does not make much sense according to the understanding I have given of the Eighth Amendment. If the amendment is designed to bring outlier states into step with a broader consensus, the consensus should presumably be among Americans. The idea behind the amendment, on this understanding, is that letting some states engage in practices that a national majority finds barbaric is bad. Allowing national values to trump local values makes good sense in such cases. But allowing foreign values to trump American values makes less sense. It is hard to 'see what is wrong with letting states engage in practices that Americans accept but foreigners do not. The Constitution does not seem concerned with bringing America into line with foreign opinion. Indeed, in some cases the Constitution requires us to depart from foreign opinion—few countries protect speech to the extent that the First Amendment does.

However, *Roper* and *Atkins* do not actually seem to be using foreign practices to decide whether a punishment is unusual. *Atkins* seems to have taken the third option, using foreign opinion as a hint to the likely future of American opinion. The existence of a foreign consensus, the Court says, "lends further support to our conclusion" that a similar consensus exists in America.[11] The reasoning here is presumably that a stable and overwhelming foreign consensus suggests that the American consensus will persist and increase. This is an appropriate use of foreign practice: it is being used as evidence to evaluate American opinion. People may disagree about its evidentiary value, but there is nothing wrong with considering it.

Roper is more troubling. The *Roper* Court chose the second option, using foreign opinion to help it decide whether a punishment is cruel. It suggested that the views of the international community should be relevant to the determination "whether the death penalty is disproportionate punishment for juveniles."[12] This issue, the majority said, is one that the Court must decide for itself, but the "opinion of the world community" provides "respected and significant confirmation for our own conclusions."[13]

Based on the account I have given of the Eighth Amendment's meaning, one might wonder why the Court has to use its "independent judgment" to decide whether a punishment is cruel or not. The cruelty analysis, I have suggested, need only consider whether the states that have abandoned a punishment have done so because they think it is too harsh. That does not call for independent judgment, only for an assessment of motives of state legislatures.

One might also wonder what the practical significance of independent judgment is. The Eighth Amendment prohibits only those punishments that are both cruel *and* unusual. Deciding that a punishment is cruel will not allow the Court to prohibit it unless a majority of states have abandoned it. If they have, it is most likely because they think it is too harsh—that is, cruel. We can imagine other circumstances—some states might abandon a punishment because it costs too much, or has proven ineffective. But in such cases there is unlikely to be an international consensus, or even a plausible argument, that the punishment is cruel. Thus, one might wonder how the exercise of independent judgment could change the outcome.

The answer to both questions is that *Roper* also suggests that the Cruel and Unusual Punishment Clause prohibits punishments that are cruel (or "disproportionate") *even if* they are not unusual. The unusual nature of a punishment is taken as evidence of disproportionality, but it is no longer a required element. If cruelty by itself is enough to strike down a punishment, and if the Court, accepting the guidance of foreign opinion, can decide for itself whether a punishment is cruel, we might justifiably worry that judges will use foreign values to displace American ones. What is troubling about *Roper,* then, is not the result. It is the suggestion that cruelty is to be determined by the Court and not by the American people.

Further Reading

Atkins and *Roper* are too recent to have been the subject of many books. On the death penalty more generally, useful sources include Stuart Banner, *The Death Penalty: An American History* (Harvard University Press, 2002); Hugo Adam Bedau and Paul Cassell, eds., *Debating the Death Penalty: Should America Have Capital Punishment?: The Experts on Both Sides Make Their Best Case* (Oxford University Press, 2003); Bill Kurtis, *The Death Penalty on Trial: Crisis in American Justice* (PublicAffairs, 2004); and Scott Turow, *Ultimate Punishment: A Lawyer's Reflections on Dealing with the Death Penalty* (Farrar, Straus and Giroux, 2003).

10

The First Amendment: Campaign Finance Reform

C oncerned about the distorting effect of money on the political process, both the federal government and the states have enacted laws that regulate political contributions and expenditures. In its early encounters with such laws, the Supreme Court displayed considerable skepticism, holding that the First Amendment invalidated many of the restrictions. In the 2003 case of *McConnell v. Federal Election Commission,* however, the Court upheld almost all of the ambitious McCain-Feingold Bipartisan Campaign Finance Reform Act.[1]

Conservatives and libertarians were dismayed. *Men in Black* discusses campaign finance reform in a chapter entitled "Silencing Political Debate." Levin calls the Court's view of free speech "absurd and dangerous," and expresses astonishment that it could uphold McCain-Feingold while not allowing states to ban flag-burning or restrict commercial speech such as tobacco advertising.[2]

The reaction is understandable, at least at a superficial level. If political speech is more important than commercial speech, it is indeed counterintuitive that the government should be able to impose greater limits on it. But closer analysis will show that the Court's approach is in fact eminently sensible.

The place to start, of course, is the First Amendment itself. The Speech Clause provides that "Congress shall make no law ... abridging the freedom of speech." But as is usually the case, the text does not take us very far. (The "plain meaning" approach that Levin favors would in fact explain the Court's decisions, since commercial advertisements are speech, while political contributions are not. But that observation really only shows yet again how pointless it is to claim that plain meaning resolves any difficult cases.) So we must decide: What counts as speech? And what counts as an abridgement?

To answer these questions, we need to have some theory about the purpose of the First Amendment. The one I will offer here is what the Supreme Court tends to endorse. Academics have come up with many others, but they overlap with this one to a substantial degree and the differences in emphasis or shading are not important here. The purpose of the First Amendment, let us suppose, is to prevent the government from interfering with the search for truth through public debate, and in particular to allow the people the ability to discuss matters relevant to the project of democratic self-governance.

This understanding suggests that speech on all topics should be protected, but that political speech is at the core of the First Amendment right. Indeed, the Court has regularly reaffirmed the centrality of such speech. It has also extended protection to nonpolitical speech, to forms of expression other than literal speech (for instance, flag-burning), and to activities essentially connected to speech (like expressive association and political contributions).

The next question is what counts as an abridgment. One

approach would be to identify all laws that by their terms restrict speech and invalidate them unless the government could show a very pressing justification. The key doctrinal question would thus be simply, "Does this law restrict speech?" Courts are as good as legislatures at answering that question, and so they should probably decide it for themselves rather than deferring to legislatures. This would produce the libertarian approach to the First Amendment, which seeks essentially to prevent all government regulation of speech. It is shared by some Supreme Court justices, and it is legitimate. But focusing on the purpose of the Speech Clause might also lead us to a different approach, one that will do a better job of promoting that purpose.

Consider first the fact that my ability to speak on political topics is not limited only by laws that explicitly prevent me from speaking. I cannot publish my views in the *New York Times* editorial page or broadcast them over the Fox News Network—at least, not unless the owners of those media outlets let me. If I want media access, I will probably have to buy it, and if I cannot afford it, I am out of luck. If I try to speak through a media entity without its owner's permission, the government will stop me. Laws that protect property have the effect of limiting my ability to speak. More generally, they ensure that those with more money will be able to speak more effectively.

Of course, those are incidental effects of good and sensible laws. We could not have a stable and productive society without protections for private property. But what makes the laws good and sensible is not that they give the wealthy a disproportionate voice. That is an unintended consequence. The set of legal rules we have has produced a situation whereby some people can speak more than others, and there is no reason to think that this situation is best in terms of facilitating the free discussion of political issues. Indeed, it seems quite likely that the greater ability of the wealthy to disseminate and advance their viewpoints will skew public debate in their favor.

If what we are concerned about is the quality of public debate, the key question is not whether a law restricts speech. It is whether it improves or worsens the conditions for public debate. Attempts to level the playing field by reducing the influence of money on the political process might well improve the quality of debate.

What this perspective reveals is that there can be such a thing as speech-friendly regulation. The libertarian understanding of the First Amendment maintains that government intervention in the marketplace of ideas is always a bad thing. But the analogy to the marketplace suggests exactly the opposite. Free markets are free *because* they are regulated—because the government enforces contracts, prohibits coercion and theft, and prevents anti-competitive practices like monopolies. Regulation to ensure a free market of ideas—for instance, to prevent the voices of those who have money from drowning out the voices of those who do not—is no more a contradiction than regulation to ensure a free market for goods and services.

From this perspective, the fact that the Court has upheld some restrictions on political speech while striking down state limits on tobacco advertising is not surprising. Speech-friendly regulation should not be considered an abridgement of the freedom of speech; it is an enhancement. Campaign finance reform is (or might be) an improvement to the conditions for speech. Restrictions on commercial advertising are not.

All this discussion works at the level of constitutional meaning. The question remains, how to translate the meaning into doctrine. In particular, should the Court defer to a legislature's conclusion that a given restriction will improve the public's ability to debate political issues?

How a law will affect the speech environment is a complicated factual question. Ordinarily, I have suggested, legislatures are better than courts at answering such questions, and courts should defer to legislative judgments. In the context of campaign finance, however, another issue is present, one which Levin, to his credit, identifies. Campaign finance regulations "are passed by the very incumbent politicians who benefit from silencing their opponents."[3] Courts must therefore be especially concerned with the possibility that such regulations will end up benefiting incumbents. On that issue, they should not defer. If no such prohibited purpose appears, however, deference is appropriate.

Further Reading

The perspective on the First Amendment I offer here is not new in legal scholarship. Notable and more thorough statements of it may be found in Owen M. Fiss's *The Irony of Free Speech* (Harvard University Press, 1996) and *Liberalism Divided: Freedom of Speech and the Many Uses of State Power* (Westview Press, 1996); and Cass R. Sunstein's *Democracy and the Problem of Free Speech* (Free Press, 1995) and *The Partial Constitution* (Harvard University Press, 1993). Stephen Breyer endorses a similar approach in *Active Liberty: Interpreting Our Democratic Constitution* (Knopf, 2005). For analysis of the First Amendment more generally, valuable resources include C. Edwin Baker's *Human Liberty and Freedom of Speech* (Oxford University Press, 1992) and *Media, Markets, and Democracy* (Cambridge University Press, 2001); Alexander Meiklejohn, *Free Speech and Its Relation to Self-Government* (Harper Brothers, 1948); and Robert Post, *Constitutional Domains: Democracy, Community, Management* (Harvard University Press, 1995).

IV
Illegitimacy

Part III discussed a number of the Court's recent and controversial cases. My argument is that these decisions are legitimate. Of course, to say that a decision is legitimate, as I have defined the term, is not saying much. It does not mean that the Constitution requires the result the Court has reached. Other approaches might also be legitimate; indeed, in some cases, other approaches might be better. It means only that the decisions can be explained and justified as sensible attempts to implement a reasonable understanding of constitutional meaning. But it is saying something, for there are also decisions whose legitimacy is much harder to establish. In Part IV I examine several cases whose legitimacy is doubtful, followed by several whose illegitimacy is generally conceded—the worst decisions the Supreme Court has ever made.

11

Refusing to Defer

In questioning the legitimacy of these decisions, I do not mean to accuse the Court of deliberately imposing its policy preferences on the nation. True activism, in that sense, is vanishingly rare. (Even *Bush v. Gore,* I will suggest, is not best understood in that light, or at least not entirely.) I mean only that the justifications offered for these decisions do not stand up to scrutiny. In most of them, the Court has made a basic conceptual mistake: it has failed to see the difference between doctrine and meaning. That failure has produced doctrine that cannot be described as a reasonable attempt to implement constitutional meaning. If we are going to complain about Supreme Court decisions, these are the ones we should be complaining about.

The Commerce Clause: *Lopez* and *Morrison*

The scope of Congress's power to legislate under the Commerce Clause is one of the more technical of the issues I discuss. It does not have the political salience of abortion, or gay rights, or affirmative action. It is quite important, however. It presents the issue of the respective authorities of the states and the federal government. More particularly, it presents the issue of which activities Congress has the power to regulate, and which must be left to the states.

The federal government is a government of enumerated powers. It can act only pursuant to the authority the Constitution gives it. If it exceeds that authority, its laws are not law at all. They cannot be enforced to deprive people of liberty or property, as the Due Process Clause confirms. The limits on federal authority are found by examining the clauses of the Constitution that grant it power. The Commerce Clause is one of the constitutional provisions that empower Congress, authorizing it "to regulate commerce with foreign nations and among the several states."

At first blush, the meaning of this clause might seem quite simple: Congress has the power to regulate interstate commerce, and nothing else. If that is the relevant meaning, there is no obvious reason that courts should defer. Whether a given activity amounts to interstate commerce is not a complicated factual question. It is a simple categorical question, and courts are as good as Congress at answering it.

In the early part of the twentieth century, the Court largely followed this understanding of the Commerce Clause. It allowed Congress to regulate commercial transactions that crossed state lines, but not activity that was purely intrastate, and it decided for itself the nature of the activity.[1] As an implementation of the Commerce Clause alone, these decisions were legitimate. They simply adopted a non-deferential doctrinal rule, which is appropriate so far as it goes given that no clear reason for deference existed.

The problem with the decisions was that they ignored

another power-granting provision of the Constitution: the Necessary and Proper Clause. This clause gives Congress the power to pass all laws "necessary and proper for carrying into execution" its enumerated powers. Adding the Necessary and Proper Clause to the analysis complicates the constitutional meaning. In addition to its direct power over interstate commerce, Congress has the power to regulate other activities if their regulation is a necessary and proper means of regulating interstate commerce. In 1937, in *National Labor Relations Board v. Jones & Laughlin Steel Corporation,* the Supreme Court recognized this. It echoed the wording of the Necessary and Proper Clause, holding that "intrastate activities that 'have such a close and substantial relationship to interstate commerce that their control is *essential* or *appropriate* to protect that commerce from burdens and obstructions' are within Congress' power to regulate."[2]

Jones & Laughlin was correct in its articulation of constitutional meaning. (Mark Levin criticizes the decision, in a chapter in *Men in Black* provocatively titled "Socialism from the Bench," but he neglects even to mention the Necessary and Proper Clause.) The next task for the Court was to fashion a doctrinal rule to implement that meaning. Whether an activity *is* interstate commerce is a question that courts can answer as well as Congress. But what *effects* an activity has on interstate commerce is not. It is a complex factual question, the sort that Congress is much better able to decide. The Court thus appropriately adopted a doctrinal rule that deferred to congressional judgment. A law would be upheld as within the commerce power if Congress could rationally have believed that the regulated activity substantially affected interstate commerce.[3]

In practical terms, given the increasing interconnections of the national economy, this meant that Congress could regulate just about anything. Between 1937 and 1995, the Court never once invalidated a law as exceeding the scope of the commerce power. In 1995, however, it did. *United States v. Lopez* struck down a federal law that criminalized the possession of guns near schools.[4]

Lopez came as a surprise, but its facts offered some justification for a less deferential approach. Whether the possession of guns near schools substantially affects interstate commerce is a question that Congress is better able to answer than a court. But the record in Lopez did not demonstrate that Congress had made an effort to answer it. It had not conducted hearings focused on that question, and it had not made any findings about the existence of such an effect. If Congress has not used the institutional capacities that make it better than the Court at answering the question, there is less reason for the Court to defer to a congressional judgment that is only implicit.

The Court might thus have been justified in attempting to decide the substantial effects question for itself, rather than asking whether Congress could rationally have found such an effect. But that is not what it did. Instead, it suggested that certain kinds of noncommercial activities were not within the power of Congress to regulate, regardless of the magnitude of their effects.

Any thought that *Lopez* turned on the absence of congressional findings was dispelled five years later. In 2000, in *United States v. Morrison,* the Court struck down part of the federal Violence Against Women Act (VAWA), which had given the victims of gender-motivated violence a federal cause of action against their attackers.[5] In the course of enacting VAWA, Congress conducted extensive hearings on the effects of gender-motivated violence on interstate commerce, and the law contained explicit findings that "crimes of violence motivated by gender have a substantial adverse effect on interstate commerce."[6] The Court ignored these findings. Expanding on *Lopez*, it announced that the commerce power did not extend to noncommercial activities that had traditionally been regulated by the states and that affected interstate commerce only indirectly.

Is this a legitimate doctrinal rule? The question in terms of meaning is whether a given activity affects interstate commerce substantially enough to make its regulation an appropriate means to the protection of commerce. In *Lopez*, I suggested, there might have been reasons for the Court to answer this question without deferring to Congress. But in *Morrison* there were not. More to the point, the rule the *Morrison* Court came up with does not attempt to answer this question in a less deferential manner. It does not attempt to answer the question at all. Instead, it creates a categorical exclusion to the commerce power, a doctrinal rule that is not connected to constitutional meaning in any obvious way unless the Necessary and Proper Clause is ignored.

Indeed, *Lopez* and *Morrison* do not try to justify their new rule by reference to the meaning of the Commerce or Necessary and Proper Clauses. Their argument appeals instead to the broader structure of the Constitution. It goes as follows: The Constitution enumerates limited powers for the federal government. There must, therefore, be activities that Congress cannot regulate under the Commerce Clause. But the pre-*Lopez* doctrinal test ("Could Congress rationally have believed that this activity substantially affects interstate commerce?") will never lead the Court to strike down a law. Therefore the doctrine must be wrong and should be changed.

There is a superficial plausibility to this argument. If Congress has enumerated powers only, it seems to follow that there must be some things it cannot regulate. (An enumeration, as the Court sometimes says, presupposes something not enumerated.) And if there are some things that Congress cannot regulate, it seems to follow that there must be laws the Court should strike down.

But in fact neither of those inferences is sound. The first is mistaken because it fails to take into account the effect of changing circumstances. The power to regulate all activity substantially affecting interstate commerce will have a limited scope in a largely agrarian society. But the development of an industrialized, integrated national economy may make the same power extend much farther.

The second mistake is the more serious one. It rests on a failure to distinguish between doctrine and meaning. Doctrine, I have said, does not track meaning perfectly. If the Court adopts a deferential doctrinal test, it will uphold laws that in fact violate the Constitution. An extremely deferential test may, in practice, not strike down any laws at all. But that does not mean that no constitutional limits exist. It simply means that courts will not enforce them, that some other branch of government has been given the primary responsibility for making sure the limits are not exceeded.

Thus, the argument that led the Court to think that it needed to change the pre-*Lopez* doctrine is simply wrong. And once we discard that argument, *Lopez* and *Morrison* have no evident justification. A basic conceptual mistake has led the Court to illegitimate results.

This mistake is not confined to the Commerce Clause. The Court has committed it repeatedly. Indeed, the failure to distinguish between doctrine and meaning is the common thread linking most of the cases I discuss in this part. The following sections will show how it plays out in other areas.

Section 5 of the Fourteenth Amendment: *Garrett* and *Kimel*

Another grant of congressional power is found in the Fourteenth Amendment. The first section of the amendment places
limits on what states can do. That section contains the Equal
Protection, Due Process, and Privileges or Immunities Clauses.
Section 5 of the amendment then provides that Congress "shall
have power to enforce, by appropriate legislation, the provisions
of this article." Just like the Commerce and Necessary and
Proper Clauses, Section 5 authorizes Congress to pass certain
laws. Just as it has in the Commerce Clause cases, the Court has
confronted the question of how to decide whether a given law
exceeds the power granted to Congress. And just as it did in
Morrison and *Lopez,* the Court has created illegitimate doctrine because of a confusion between doctrine and meaning.

The scope of the Section 5 enforcement power is one of
the most complex and technical issues in constitutional law. It
is certainly the most technical of the ones I discuss. And until
recently, it seemed to have little practical significance. Since the
commerce power seemed to allow Congress to pass almost any
law it wanted, the question of whether those laws might also be
justified by Section 5 was purely academic.

The scope of Section 5 is worth discussing here for several reasons, however. First, it provides a tidy illustration of the
consequences of failing to distinguish doctrine from meaning.
But it is also an increasingly important question. The Court's
recent and more restrictive reading of the Commerce Clause
raises the possibility that some laws will survive judicial review
only if they can be based on the Section 5 power.

Additionally, change in another doctrinal area has brought
Section 5 to the foreground. Over the past ten years, the Court

has grown increasingly solicitous of what it terms the "dignity" of the states. This concern has led it to create a doctrine of state sovereign immunity. That is another extremely technical area of law, but the basic point is easy to grasp. The Court has held that Congress cannot use the commerce power to authorize individuals to sue states for money damages. Only laws based on the Section 5 power can pierce state sovereign immunity in that way. Thus, the ability of individuals such as state employees to win money damages for violations of federal civil rights laws, or minimum wage requirements, depends on whether those laws can be justified as exercises of the power granted by Section 5.

Determining the scope of the Section 5 power requires us first to decide what it means to "enforce" the Fourteenth Amendment. The Court has consistently maintained that to enforce means to deter or remedy state acts that violate the amendment. If Congress goes beyond deterring or remedying violations, however, and tries to change the *meaning* of the Fourteenth Amendment by ordinary legislation, it has gone too far. Having settled on that understanding of constitutional meaning, the Court confronted two questions in creating doctrine. First, how deferential should the Court be in deciding whether a particular law is "appropriate" to deter or remedy a state violation? Second, and more important, how should the Court decide what counts as a violation?

The first question has not proved especially controversial. In granting Congress the power to pass "appropriate" legislation, Section 5 echoes the Necessary and Proper Clause, which the Court has consistently read to give Congress broad discretion. A deferential stance also makes obvious sense. Deciding what will be the most effective way to deter or remedy violations of the Fourteenth Amendment involves the sort of complex factual analysis that Congress can perform better than courts. The Court has required enforcement legislation to be "congruent and proportional" to the violations it counters, a standard which it has stated gives Congress "wide latitude" in choosing enforcement measures.[7]

It is the second question that has turned out to be crucial. The congruence and proportionality standard measures enforcement legislation against the violations it seeks to deter or remedy. It asks whether Congress has prohibited an excessive number of state acts that do not violate the Fourteenth Amendment. If so, the effect of the legislation is not so much to enforce the Fourteenth Amendment as to change and expand it. Such a law is disproportionate to the violations and will be struck down. But that leaves open the question of what counts as a violation. In particular, it does not decide whether the state act must violate the *meaning* of the Fourteenth Amendment, or the *doctrine* that the Court has created to implement that meaning.

Suppose that Congress has prohibited employment discrimination on the basis of age and disability. (That is what it did in the cases I will discuss.) The meaning of the Equal Protection Clause, I have said, is that states may not engage in unjustified discrimination. If the Court measures Congress's laws against meaning, it will ask whether Congress is reacting to *unjustified* state discrimination on the basis of age and disability. And given that legislatures are generally better than courts at balancing costs and benefits, the Court will probably defer to a congressional determination that discrimination is unjustified.

If the Court is measuring the laws against doctrine, however, the analysis will be very different. As I described in chapter 2, the Court does not decide equal protection cases just by

asking whether a particular act of discrimination is unjustified. Instead, it sorts discrimination into different categories.
Most discrimination is reviewed very deferentially. It will be
upheld if it is rationally related to a legitimate state interest.
The basic reason for this deferential review is the one mentioned in the preceding paragraph: representative bodies like
legislatures are better than courts at deciding complex factual
questions and balancing competing values, able to correct
their mistakes, and accountable to voters if they do not.

Discrimination based on certain characteristics, like race,
is treated differently. But age and disability are not among those
characteristics. A court will not strike down discrimination
against the elderly or the disabled unless it is irrational. So if
the Court is measuring Congress's laws against doctrine, it will
ask if Congress is reacting to *irrational* state discrimination on
the basis of age and disability. Deciding whether discrimination is irrational does not require a difficult balancing of costs
and benefits or the reconciliation of deeply contested competing values. It is a task that courts can perform—indeed, it is
precisely because courts can answer that question that it makes
a sensible doctrinal test. So the Court will also be less likely to
defer to a congressional judgment that states are discriminating irrationally.

Which approach is the correct one? If the question is
phrased in this way, the answer is obvious. The concern, after
all, is that if Congress goes too far, it effectively changes the
meaning of the amendment. Thus, the violations that are relevant are violations of constitutional meaning, not doctrine.
Whether Congress has effectively changed the Court's doctrine
is not really relevant. That doctrine is tailored to accommodate
the respective abilities of federal courts and state legislatures.
Congress's institutional capacities are those of a legislature,

not a court, and there is no reason to think that rules the Court has adopted for its own use will necessarily be appropriate for Congress.

Through the latter part of the twentieth century, the Court seemed to understand this point. It upheld enforcement legislation if it was an appropriate response to state practices that violated constitutional meaning. When Congress acted to enforce the Equal Protection Clause, for instance, the Court determined the existence of a violation by asking whether Congress might reasonably have found that state discrimination was unjustified (or "invidious"). It did not ask whether the Court itself would hold the state action unconstitutional. As Justice Brennan explained in 1966, "it is enough that we perceive a basis upon which Congress might predicate a judgment" that the state act violated the Equal Protection Clause.[8]

Recently, however, at much the same time as it was announcing new restrictions on the commerce power, the Court lost sight of the distinction. In *Board of Trustees of the University of Alabama v. Garrett*,[9] dealing with the Americans with Disabilities Act, and *Kimel v. Florida Board of Regents*,[10] dealing with the Age Discrimination in Employment Act, the Court held that Congress had exceeded the scope of the Section 5 power.

These laws prohibit employers from discriminating on the basis of age or disability, and they allow injured individuals to sue for money damages. In each case, the plaintiffs were state employees seeking to recover damages from their employers. As applied to private employers, the laws were clearly valid exercises of the commerce power. But because of the Court's decision that the commerce power could not authorize money damages against states, the suits against state employers could go forward only if the anti-discrimination laws were appropriate measures to enforce the Equal Protection Clause.

Garrett and *Kimel* clearly measure congressional enforcement legislation against doctrine, rather than meaning. In *Kimel,* the Court began by reciting its doctrinal rule: "States may discriminate on the basis of age without offending the Fourteenth Amendment if the age classification in question is rationally related to a legitimate state interest." It went on to measure the Age Discrimination in Employment Act "against the rational basis standard of our equal protection jurisprudence."[11] Because the act "prohibits substantially more state employment decisions and practices than would likely be held unconstitutional under the applicable equal protection, rational basis standard," the Court found that it crossed the boundary from enforcement legislation to an impermissible "attempt to substantively redefine the States' legal obligations."[12]

Garrett offers an even sharper display of the assumption that doctrine and meaning are the same thing. The opinion comes very close to saying that discrimination based on hostility or stereotypes against the disabled is constitutionally acceptable. The Court observed that although "negative attitudes may often accompany irrational (and therefore unconstitutional) discrimination, their presence alone does not a constitutional violation make."[13] In deciding whether Congress had prohibited too many constitutionally acceptable state practices, the Court compared the outcome of litigation under the Americans with Disabilities Act to the outcome of litigation under the Equal Protection Clause, right down to such technical doctrinal matters as the allocation of the burden of proof.[14]

If doctrine and meaning were the same thing, the results in *Garrett* and *Kimel* would make sense. But they are not. And once we get past that conceptual mistake, the justification for the Court's approach disappears. There is no obvious reason why enforcement legislation should be measured against the rules that the Court has adopted to guide its own decision-making, and the Court has never tried to offer one. Once again, conceptual confusion has led to illegitimate results.

Affirmative Action: From *Bakke* to *Grutter*

Neither the Commerce Clause nor Section 5 occupies a very prominent place in the public mind. But the mistake I have been discussing is not limited to arcane and technical constitutional matters. Its effects can also be seen in the Court's analysis of a divisive social issue: affirmative action.

Affirmative action, generally speaking, is the granting of benefits or preferential treatment to racial minorities. In recent history, the practice began in the 1960s. It was quickly attacked as reverse discrimination, and in 1978, in *Regents of the University of California v. Bakke,* the Supreme Court weighed in.[15]

The plaintiff was Alan Bakke, a white male who had twice been refused admission to the University of California (Davis) medical school. The Davis admissions program reserved sixteen of the one hundred places in the entering class for racial minorities whose applications demonstrated "economic or educational deprivation."[16] Bakke argued that this system violated the Equal Protection Clause.

The Supreme Court's decision in *Bakke* did not produce a majority opinion on that key question. Justice Lewis Powell's opinion, however, staked out a middle ground between the other justices, and it was generally taken as controlling. Justice Powell first decided that affirmative action should be reviewed in the same way as segregation, or other discrimination against racial minorities. Discrimination against racial minorities, I have already explained, is reviewed under the "strict scrutiny" standard. It will be upheld only if it is narrowly tailored to serve a compelling state interest.

Application of strict scrutiny almost always results in the invalidation of the government act under review, and *Bakke* proved no exception. The Court struck down the Davis admissions program. However, Justice Powell suggested that other programs might fare differently. The attainment of a diverse student body, he wrote, was a compelling state interest. State schools could consider race as one of many factors in order "to select those students who will contribute the most to the 'robust exchange of ideas.'"[17]

In response to *Bakke*, most schools revised their admissions programs along the lines that Justice Powell had indicated would be acceptable. And when the Supreme Court revisited the issue in 2003, it followed the analysis of *Bakke*.

Two 2003 cases presented challenges to the University of Michigan's admissions programs for undergraduates and law students. This time, Justice Sandra Day O'Connor assumed the centrist role Powell had played in *Bakke*. In *Gratz v. Bollinger*, the case about undergraduate admissions, she joined four justices in voting to strike down the program.[18] But in *Grutter v. Bollinger*, the law school case, she joined four other justices in voting to uphold the program.[19] The difference she found relevant (which no other justice did) was that the law school program allowed for individualized consideration and did not assign race a fixed weight in the admissions calculus.

Focusing on that difference made the Court's decisions follow public opinion, which generally supports affirmative action as long as it is not used in an obvious or mechanical way. Whether individualized consideration should make a constitutional difference is another question. Even under the law school program, race will be the decisive factor in some cases. If the Constitution prohibits treating people differently because of their race, it is hard to see why individualized consideration should matter. Conversely, if it is permissible for race to play a decisive role, it is hard to see why it cannot be given a fixed weight.

But my focus here is not the specifics of *Gratz* and *Grutter*. It is the more basic question of whether the Court's doctrine is legitimate: whether strict scrutiny of affirmative action makes sense. Assume for now that the meaning of the Equal Protection Clause is that states may not engage in unjustified discrimination. (I will consider objections to this understanding later.) The doctrine that the Court has created implements that meaning by granting different measures of deference to different kinds of discrimination. Generally speaking, it defers when there is no reason to doubt the state actor's ability to balance costs and benefits accurately. It refuses to defer, sometimes to the extent of employing the anti-deferential strict scrutiny, when such reasons do exist. The factors that lead to skepticism are things such as a history of discrimination against the group whose interests are burdened, or a lack of political power on the part of that group—things that might predictably lead a legislature to count that group's interests less heavily.

From this perspective, strict scrutiny for affirmative action is illegitimate. There is very little reason to think that state legislatures or university administrators will discount the interests of white applicants. (Perhaps the strongest argument is that the costs of affirmative action tend to fall on poorer whites, whose political power is lesser. It is certainly true that the admissions process is currently skewed in favor of the wealthy, who can afford expensive test preparation classes, but affirmative action still disadvantages wealthy white applicants.)

There is very little reason to think that they will not balance costs and benefits accurately and in good faith. And if they make a mistake, there is very little reason to think that the democratic political process will be unable to correct it. Precisely the factors that make strict scrutiny appropriate for laws that disadvantage minorities make it inappropriate for affirmative action.

At least, that is so if the meaning of the Equal Protection Clause is indeed a ban on unjustified discrimination. One way to defend the Court's approach would be to argue that the meaning is different, that it is what we could call "color blindness"— a ban on all racial discrimination.

This proposition is often asserted. Mark Levin writes that "[t]he Fourteenth Amendment prohibits all discrimination based on race, without exception."[20] Justice Clarence Thomas has said much the same thing: "What the Equal Protection Clause does prohibit are classifications made on the basis of race."[21]

But assertion is not argument. If we confine ourselves to the words of the Constitution, what Levin calls the "clear language"[22] of the Equal Protection Clause, the assertion is flatly wrong. The clause simply prohibits states from denying people "the equal protection of the laws." It does not say anything to mark race as special. Had the Congress that drafted the Equal Protection Clause wanted to prohibit all racial discrimination, it could very easily have said so. It did just that in the Fifteenth Amendment, providing that the right to vote shall not be abridged "on account of race, color, or previous condition of servitude."

Perhaps history supports the color blindness understanding? Of course, there is no denying that racial discrimination was the prime concern of the drafters of the Fourteenth

Amendment. Some form of racial discrimination, anyway—
the discrimination practiced in the South against the newly
freed slaves. But what was it about that discrimination that the
drafters found objectionable? Was it just the differential treatment on the basis of race, or was it that the differential treatment was designed to subjugate and oppress a population only
recently released from bondage?

There is no doubt that the oppressive nature of the discrimination was a concern. As the Supreme Court put it in the
Slaughterhouse Cases in 1873, the "one pervading purpose" of
the Fourteenth Amendment was "the protection of the newly-
made freeman and citizen from the oppressions of those who
had formerly exercised dominion over him."[23] There is also
little doubt that the drafters did not find racial discrimination
objectionable in and of itself. When Mark Levin states that
"'[a]ffirmative action' has been around since the 1960s,"[24] he is
off by a hundred years. The same Congress that drafted the
Equal Protection Clause repeatedly enacted racially discriminatory laws, in order to benefit racial minorities. (For instance,
it several times enacted laws providing money for the relief of
destitute "colored" persons.[25]) Faced with this historical evidence, it is hard to argue that the original understanding of the
Equal Protection Clause prohibited all racial discrimination
across the board.

One might still argue that the clause is designed to prohibit "unjust" discrimination, discrimination that offends our
notions of fairness. This would not be an originalist approach, but the champions of originalism show surprisingly
little interest in the history surrounding the Equal Protection
Clause when it comes to affirmative action. And one might
then argue that racial discrimination is unjust because it
treats people differently based on characteristics over which

they have no control, and that are unrelated to any reasonable understanding of merit.

That is true enough. Affirmative action, like discrimination against racial minorities, conflicts with a basic notion of fairness, the principle that people should be judged only on their merits as individuals. But if the Equal Protection Clause enacted that principle, courts would be very busy indeed. They would be busy, for starters, invalidating geographic preferences and preferences for alumni children. In the end, judicial enforcement of some intuitive notion of fairness would represent a stunning incursion on the ability of elected government bodies to make policy choices. The Court has never asserted the power to do this; it recognizes that the ordinary remedy for unjust laws is the democratic process.

So none of these arguments works. Perhaps for that reason, the Court has not relied on any of them. Instead, when it does offer an argument, it tends to resort to the fundamental principle that equal protection must protect everyone equally. As Justice Powell put it in *Bakke*, in language the Court would quote repeatedly, "[t]he guarantee of equal protection cannot mean one thing when applied to one individual and something else when applied to a person of another color. If both are not accorded the same protection, then it is not equal."[26]

The principle is undeniable. But it is a principle about the meaning of the Equal Protection Clause, and it is readily satisfied by an understanding on which all people are equally protected against unjustified discrimination. The Court seems to suppose that it must apply equally to doctrine, or rather, that doctrine is the same thing as meaning. And that, of course, is not true. Doctrine is a set of rules designed to respond to particular circumstances. If affirmative action differs from discrimination against racial minorities in terms of how it has been used historically, or whether legislatures can be trusted to assess costs and benefits accurately, doctrine will differ too.

So again, the confusion between doctrine and meaning has led the Court to create doctrine that has no evident justification. By saying that strict scrutiny for affirmative action is illegitimate, I am not saying that affirmative action is just, or fair, or a good policy choice. It might be none of those things. I am saying only that its costs and benefits can be left to the democratic political process. There is no reason to think that the people, through their representatives, cannot deal with affirmative action appropriately, and there is no reason to take the decision away from them.

There is one more point that should be made. Affirmative action may be just or unjust; I take no position on that question. But I do assert that taking the issue of affirmative action away from the political process is unjust.

This becomes clear if we stop to think about the consequences. Under the Court's approach to equal protection, most sorts of preferential treatment are allowed. The government may grant subsidies to farmers, married couples, or the unemployed; public universities can adopt preferential admission policies for athletes, flautists, alumni children, or applicants from remote geographical regions. Racial minorities, almost alone, cannot be favored.

The reason for this is not that racial discrimination is especially unfair in terms of rewarding irrelevant characteristics—from that perspective, it is no less fair than granting preferences to alumni children. The reason that race is constitutionally special is simple. We had slavery. We had the Black Codes, systematic attempts to deprive the freed slaves of civil rights. We had Jim Crow, and segregation. We had rampant discrimination against immigrants of different races. Race is special because until relatively recently, American history was a long and consistent tale of oppression of racial minorities. But to turn this into an argument against affirmative action is to say that the reason racial minorities cannot be favored now is because they were discriminated against in the past.

When you put it in those terms, it should be relatively clear that this does not make much sense. In fact, the Supreme Court has said so. In *Romer v. Evans,* remember, the Court struck down a Colorado constitutional amendment that barred gays and lesbians from securing protection under local anti-discrimination ordinances. Such an exclusion of a group from the ordinary play of politics was "unprecedented in our jurisprudence," Justice Kennedy wrote, "a denial of equal protection in its most literal sense," and "inexplicable as anything but animus."[27] Some of that may be true, but not the unprecedented part. This prohibition on using the political process to gain advantage is exactly what current equal protection jurisprudence does to racial minorities.

Fighting Activism: *Bush v. Gore*

Thus far, the illegitimate decisions I have identified have a common source in the failure to distinguish between doctrine and meaning. Calling these decisions illegitimate is certainly a criticism. It is a criticism of the doctrine: I think that the doctrine is unjustifiable and the Court should change it. It is also a criticism of the Court, in a way: I think the Court has made a conceptual mistake. But I am not saying that the Court has done this deliberately, that it has knowingly chosen unjustifiable doctrine in order to promote policies the justices favor. I accuse the Court of intellectual sloppiness, not bad faith.

Something else was going on in *Bush v. Gore*. It was not intellectual sloppiness; the justices knew what they were doing. Many commentators assume that bad faith, in the form of a desire to see George W. Bush elected, is the only other explanation. That is an easy conclusion to draw, and at some moments I have shared it. But in the end I think that *Bush v. Gore* has something else to teach us.

So much has been written about the election of 2000 that any further discussion may seem redundant. It might also seem to come too late to be of any use. We have had other things to think about since then, and America, by and large, has moved on. I will try to show, however, that *Bush v. Gore* is relevant to the continuing debate over judicial activism—and in a surprising way.

The context of that decision is no doubt familiar. My account here is streamlined, but it presents the crucial facts. As Election Night 2000 turned into the morning of November 8, Florida remained too close to call. Bush and Gore stood together on the brink of victory; whichever candidate received Florida's twenty-five electoral votes would win the election. When the vote tally was completed on November 8, Bush held a slim lead of 1,784 votes. This was less than 0.5 percent of the votes cast, and Florida law therefore directed an automatic recount. The recount shrank Bush's lead to 327 votes.

Gore's legal team decided that their most promising strategy was to seek hand recounts in selected counties that used punch-card voting machines. Punch-card machines require voters to punch a small piece of paper, called a chad, out of the ballot. The ballot is then read by a machine that shines light through it to determine which chads have been punched. Vote tallies in punch-card counties showed a surprising number of undervotes—ballots on which no vote had been cast for a presidential candidate. Gore's lawyers reasoned that application of Florida's legal standard for counting a vote (whether the intent of the voter could be clearly discerned) would reveal that a substantial number of undervotes did contain votes for president—and, since the lawyers had selected counties Gore won, that the discovery of these votes would help Gore more than Bush.

Some counties completed hand recounts; some did not, even after the Florida Supreme Court extended the initial deadline for the county canvassing boards to submit their results. On November 26, Secretary of State Katherine Harris certified Bush as the winner of the popular vote by 537 votes. The next day, Gore began the election "contest" authorized by Florida law by filing suit in a Florida state court. The case eventually reached the Florida Supreme Court. On December 8, that court ordered that the results of the hand recounts completed after the deadline, or partially completed, be included in the tally, shrinking Bush's lead to 154. It also ordered a statewide hand recount of all undervotes, which amounted to some 60,000 ballots.

The Florida Supreme Court did not, however, specify any precise test by which to determine whether an undervote should be counted. Undervoted ballots might show several different features arguably suggesting the intent to cast a vote. A chad might be partially detached, but still adhering to the ballot. It might be dimpled, showing that the voter pressed on it, but did not detach it. It might have a small hole, showing that the voter broke through the chad without detaching it. As the statewide hand recount began, county canvassing boards adopted different standards for what counted as adequate evidence of the intent to cast a vote.

Bush's lawyers had meanwhile sought review by the federal Supreme Court, something the Court had discretion to grant or deny. On December 9, the Court granted review and issued a stay, halting the recounts until it decided the case. Late at night on December 11, the Court issued its opinion, holding that the application of different standards to determine the intent of the voter violated the Equal Protection Clause. A recount with consistent standards, the opinion suggested, would be constitutionally permissible. But Florida law, the Court asserted, required final submission of the results by December 12. Since it was plainly impossible to complete a statewide recount with consistent standards by that date, the Court's opinion also stated that no further recount was permissible. And as everyone knows, the vote tally that proved decisive was five to four, splitting the Court along its standard liberal-conservative line.

Few commentators found the equal protection argument persuasive. (Interestingly, Justices Stephen Breyer and David Souter did; their dissenting opinions agreed that the disparate standards created a constitutional problem, though they would have allowed the Florida Supreme Court to attempt to fix it.) There are, I think, two basic objections to it. First, as a general principle, it goes much too far. The equal protection concern is that different standards in different counties will in practice lead to different treatment of identical votes. The same ballot would be considered a valid vote in one county but not in another, and therefore it will effectively be easier to vote in one county than another.

That certainly seems like something to worry about— except that it's the way things work in elections. Different counties regularly use different methods of voting, and these methods produce different rates of invalid ballots. That is, it is easier to cast a valid vote in some counties than in others. In

Florida, in the election of 2000, for instance, twenty-four counties used punch cards. This system resulted in a spoilage rate of 3.9 percent. Twenty-four used optical scanning, coupled with a system that immediately informed the voter if the ballot could not be read and allowed another attempt. This system produced a 0.6 percent spoilage rate. And in the fifteen counties that used optical scanning without a second chance, 5.7 percent of ballots were invalid.[28] (The notorious "butterfly ballot," which apparently led many Palm Beach voters to mistakenly cast ballots for Patrick Buchanan when they intended to vote for Gore, is another example, though its effects are probably impossible to quantify objectively.)

The Court's equal protection rationale would seem to suggest that these sorts of variations also presented a constitutional problem. It was presumably to avert that suggestion that the Court explicitly announced that its reasoning was "limited to the present circumstances."[29] The doctrine announced in *Bush v. Gore,* then, is not to be considered generally applicable.

The second problem with the Court's equal protection rationale is that the Court seemed not to consider how its solution stacked up against the one the Florida Supreme Court had ordered. Assuming that a single standard for determining the intent of the voter was required, the different standards applied in the hand recounts were producing errors. They were either counting some votes that should not have been counted, or they were failing to count some that should have been, depending on what the "correct" standard is deemed to be. But the Court's solution also produced errors, of course. By stopping all the recounts, it almost certainly produced *more* errors, regardless of what the correct standard might have been. Under the correct standard, that is, all of the machine-readable votes were legally valid, and so were the ones that were not

machine-readable but met the standard. Yet the Court effectively ordered that all of the valid but not machine-readable
votes be discarded. That seems more like the creation of an
equal protection problem than its solution.

The two problems with the Court's approach can be described in similar terms from the perspective of doctrine and
meaning. At the level of meaning, there is very little controversy. The Equal Protection Clause entitles voters to identical
treatment unless some adequate justification exists. The key
question in *Bush v. Gore* was who could be trusted to decide
justifiable kinds of differential treatment. On this doctrinal
question, the Court took an anti-deferential approach in a situation where deference is the norm and the benefits of an anti-
deferential approach are not obvious. It refused to leave the
setting of standards for evaluating ballots up to county boards,
even though courts generally decline to second-guess the justification for similar county-by-county variations. And it refused to allow the Florida Supreme Court to deal with the
problem of ignoring valid votes, even though state courts usually receive deference in their application of state law and the
U.S. Supreme Court's solution was not obviously better than
that of the Florida court.

Why would the Court adopt doctrine that has these
problems? It might simply have thought they were not, in fact,
problems, but that seems unlikely. The express limitation of
the rationale to "the present circumstances" indicates that the
Court did not think its approach was sound as a general matter.

The more common explanation offered is that the Court
felt it had to act to avert a constitutional crisis. Allowing the recounts to continue might have produced a situation in which
the Florida Supreme Court would end up pronouncing Gore
the winner, while the Republican-controlled Florida legisla-

ture would announce that Bush had won and invoke a provision in the federal Electoral Count Act of 1887 that allows state legislatures to specify the manner of appointing electors if the state fails to make a choice on Election Day. Different branches of the Florida government might have certified two different slates of electors. Congress would ultimately have had to choose between them under another provision of the Electoral Count Act authorizing Congress to reject electoral votes that are not "regularly given." The Senate was split 50–50 between Democrats and Republicans, and Al Gore, as the sitting vice-president, held the tiebreaking vote. The House was controlled by Republicans. Resolution by Congress might thus have been quite messy. And so, the reasoning goes, the Court felt it necessary to stop the recounts and was willing to grasp an unpersuasive legal justification if nothing better was available.

There is probably some truth to this explanation. Many commentators seemed to assume that it was appropriate and inevitable that the Court would ultimately decide the election. (That view was less common among law professors, who were generally surprised that the Court agreed to hear the case at all.) But a troubling question remains: if the situation had been reversed, if Gore had been ahead and Bush the one seeking recounts, would the same five justices have intervened to stop them?

In all fairness, I think the answer to this question has to be no. In the many books on *Bush v. Gore,* one can certainly find defenders of the decision, either as simply legally correct, or as necessary even if unconvincing. But I have not seen anyone willing to argue that the five justices in the majority would have gone to the same lengths to ensure that Al Gore would become president. As a counterfactual speculation, this would be impossible to disprove. One could assert it without embarrassment as long as it was not completely and obviously implausible on its face. The fact that I have not seen such an assertion tends to confirm my suspicion that it is, in fact, that implausible.

That means that the pragmatic explanation of the decision as necessary to ward off a constitutional crisis cannot be a full justification. Does it make the decision illegitimate?

Perhaps surprisingly, I think the answer to this question is also no. A decision is legitimate, I have said, if the doctrinal rule it applies is a reasonable way to implement a reasonable understanding of the relevant constitutional meaning. We should be asking, in other words, what reasons there are to think that the rule is a good way to achieve compliance with the underlying meaning.

What the Court did in *Bush v. Gore* was to adopt a very aggressive doctrinal rule to implement the meaning of the Equal Protection Clause—a more aggressive rule than settled law suggested was appropriate, and a more aggressive rule than the Court itself seemed to think would be appropriate in the future. The rule it chose seems to go beyond constitutional meaning; it will strike down state acts that do not, in fact, amount to unjustified discrimination. The basic reason for adopting that kind of anti-deferential stance, I have said, is that the Court does not trust the state actor whose decision it is reviewing. In the ordinary case, that would be a state legislature deciding to treat one class of people differently from another. Here, however, it was primarily the Florida Supreme Court.

That the five-justice majority did not trust the Florida Supreme Court was fairly clear. And this distrust actually explains the equal protection rationale quite well. It answers both of the objections I raised earlier. The general variation in voting procedures from county to county is attributable to other actors, so the sort of anti-deferential review the Court gave the Florida Supreme Court's decision should not logically extend to that problem, or to future cases. (It is, however, something we should worry about as citizens. Different rates of spoiled ballots correlate with wealth and with race; minority voters in Florida in 2000 saw their votes rejected at ten times the rate of white voters.[30]) And the Supreme Court's resolution looks much better compared to that of the Florida court if we suppose that the Florida court had partisan and improper purposes. The Florida court's solution, from that perspective, was not making things better; it was making them worse, and wiping it out was an improvement.

Bush v. Gore might be a legitimate decision, then, as long as we agree that the Florida Supreme Court deserved to be regarded with that kind of suspicion. The justices in the majority could have pointed to two factors that supported their view. Some form of defects in democracy existed, they could have claimed, because the Florida Supreme Court was controlled by Democratic appointees. And for the lessons of history, they could have pointed to that court's decision in *Bush v. Gore* itself, which they evidently thought was a prime example of judicial activism.

Trying to decide whether the Florida court was in fact acting in a partisan and lawless manner would take us deep into the thicket of Florida election law. And it would probably not change anyone's mind: conservatives tend to think the Florida court was partisan, and liberals think it was not. That, ultimately, is all we need to know, because it demonstrates the key point: perceptions of appropriate judicial behavior are invariably affected by ideology.

Granting that, what follows? It is in part in order to prevent judges from changing the level of deference in response to their own case-by-case evaluation of other government actors that we value consistency of doctrine. If the Court's doctrine says that state courts are generally to be trusted in the application of state law, or that county-by-county variations in voting procedures generally do not create equal protection problems, judges should not make exceptions for particular cases in which they think the state courts or county canvassing boards are acting in a partisan fashion. Evaluating the good faith of those state actors in individual cases—as distinct from the broader issue of whether such courts or boards can *generally* be trusted—is something that judges are not necessarily good at doing. Judges' views of the world, like those of everyone else, are tinged by ideology, and their assessment of good faith in an individual case is inevitably affected by their sentiments about the result. Thus, when possible, judges should structure their analysis so that it does not turn on the kinds of case-specific assessments over which ideology exerts an influence.

This conclusion applies to the rest of us as well. We have a duty to evaluate the Supreme Court's decisions, but we should try to do so in a manner that does not come down to the question of whether we find those decisions politically desirable. Asking whether the decisions reflect a reasonable and consistent response to the presence or absence of the factors I have identified is a relatively ideologically neutral way to do so. The fact that some particular decision strikes us as politically undesirable should not override the factor-based analysis. When confronted with such a decision, we should hesitate to conclude that judges are acting in bad faith. We should hesitate, too, to suppose that extraordinary measures are necessary or appropriate to curb runaway courts. *Bush v. Gore* makes sense only if the justices in the majority did both those things, and if they did, they chose a cure worse than the disease. Had the Supreme Court left the election to be settled in Congress, we might have had a more satisfying resolution. We would, at any rate, have had the decision made by officials that voters could hold to account. *Bush v. Gore* was an unfortunate over-reaction to perceived judicial activism, a self-inflicted wound for the Supreme Court.

We should be wary of inflicting such wounds ourselves. As Justice Louis Brandeis wrote, "Men feared witches and burned women."[31] A nation that fears activist judges may cripple an honest judiciary. As chapter 13 argues, that would be a terrible mistake. An independent judiciary is tremendously valuable and ours, on balance, has served us well. That is not to say the Court has been perfect. The next chapter will examine some of its more notable failures. These are the decisions that everyone, or almost everyone, agrees are wrong. Finding a common identifying feature might allow us to distill the essence of improper judicial decision-making.

Further Reading

In the Commerce Clause and Section 5 contexts, the decisions I have discussed seemed to herald a surprising narrowing of federal power. Academic reaction was generally critical. A good example is John T. Noonan, *Narrowing the Nation's Power: The Supreme Court Sides with the States* (University of California Press, 2002). A more enthusiastic view of the "New Federalism" is Michael Greve, *Real Federalism: Why It Matters, How It Could Happen* (American Enterprise Institute Press, 1999). Larry Kramer, in *The People Themselves: Popular Constitutionalism and Judicial Review* (Oxford University Press, 2004) criticizes the decisions on grounds similar to those I offer: that the

Supreme Court is aggressively enforcing the idea that it alone is entitled to interpret the Constitution.

Recent developments suggest that the New Federalism may not be the revolution it once seemed. In *Raich v. Gonzales,* 125 S.Ct. 2195 (2005), the Court upheld federal commerce power to ban the possession of home-grown medical marijuana, a decision that many observers found inconsistent with *Morrison* and *Lopez.* In *Tennessee v. Lane,* 541 U.S. 509 (2004), and *Nevada Department of Human Resources v. Hibbs,* 541 U.S. 509 (2003), the Court found that the Section 5 power allowed Congress to ensure access to public facilities for people with disabilities and to require states to grant employees leave for family and medical reasons. These decisions suggested a broader view of the Section 5 power than had *Garrett* and *Kimel.*

The constitutionality of affirmative action has been debated for a long time, and *Gratz* and *Grutter* have ensured that the issue will stay alive for a while longer. Useful contributions include Terry Eastland, *Ending Affirmative Action: The Case for Colorblind Justice* (Basic Books, 1996); Christopher Edley, *Not All Black and White: Affirmative Action and American Values* (Farrar, Straus, and Giroux, 1998). Much of the debate focuses on the moral soundness or practical consequences of affirmative action, which I view as largely irrelevant to the constitutional question of whether the choice can be left with representative institutions. Readers interested in dueling data can consult Thomas Sowell, *Affirmative Action Around the World: An Empirical Study* (Yale University Press, 2004) and William G. Bowen and Derek Bok, *The Shape of the River* (Princeton University Press, 1998). A recent contribution offering a valuable historic study of admissions practices at elite universities is Jerome Karabel, *The Chosen: The Hidden History of Admis-*

sion and Exclusion at Harvard, Yale, and Princeton (Houghton Mifflin, 2005).

With respect to the constitutional question, I should admit that in arguing for deferential review I take an extreme position. Even liberal justices like William Brennan and Thurgood Marshall have supported some form of heightened scrutiny for race-based affirmative action programs. One could argue for less deferential review on the grounds that government use of racial classifications tends to inflict high costs on society generally because it is divisive, or that it stigmatizes its beneficiaries or harms them in some other way. I do not see why legislatures or administrators cannot be trusted to make these decisions. One could also, as I mention in the text, point out that the individuals who bear the costs of affirmative action programs frequently are poor. Legislators or university administrators may be confident that their own children can achieve high enough test scores to be admitted anyway, and the children of administrators may receive admissions preferences of their own. I think these concerns are weightier, but I do not see why they justify singling out race alone as an impermissible basis for preference.

Many books have been written about *Bush v. Gore*. If you are interested in the case, you have probably read some already. Jeffrey Toobin's *Too Close to Call: The Thirty-Six-Day Battle to Decide the 2000 Election* (Random House, 2001) describes the events in Florida. For more narrowly focused commentary on the Court's performance, mostly critical, readers may be interested in Bruce Ackerman, ed., *Bush v. Gore: The Question of Legitimacy* (Yale University Press, 2001); Alan Dershowitz, *Supreme Injustice: How the High Court Hijacked Election 2000* (Oxford University Press, 2001); Howard Gillman, *The Votes That Counted: How the Court Decided the 2000 Presidential*

Election (University of Chicago Press, 2001); and Richard Epstein and Cass Sunstein, eds., *The Vote: Bush, Gore, and the Supreme Court* (University of Chicago Press, 2001).

Although some of the essays in the Ackerman and Epstein and Sunstein volumes defend the decision, the most notable defense of the Court is probably Richard Posner, *Breaking the Deadlock: The 2000 Election, the Constitution, and the Courts* (Princeton University Press, 2001).

12

Reviled Decisions

I ended the last chapter by suggesting that perceptions of appropriate judicial behavior are affected by ideology, and that this fact should lead us to hesitate before denouncing as illegitimate decisions with which we disagree. Instead, I have argued for a standard under which a decision is legitimate if it starts with a plausible understanding of constitutional meaning (seldom a deeply controversial issue) and creates sensible doctrine to implement that meaning (a question that typically comes down to what factors suggest that the Court should defer, or not defer, to another governmental actor). This approach is not perfectly objective, but it frames the analysis in terms less influenced by partisan politics.

In this chapter, I consider an alternative. There are some Supreme Court decisions that everyone agrees are bad. If we can find some common failings in those decisions, perhaps that will provide a different or better method to identify illegitimacy going forward. To that end, I discuss four decisions that modern opinion has turned against, decisions that are considered the quintessence of bad judging. Some of them, I will suggest, are not as bad as they might seem at first. Taken together, they may offer some guidance to judges. But they do not produce a principle that can lead to objective diagnoses of illegitimacy.

Resolving a Crisis: *Dred Scott v. Sandford*

Everyone knows that *Dred Scott* is a bad decision. It is perhaps the worst one ever rendered by the Supreme Court. It makes Mark Levin's list of landmark activism, along with *Plessy v. Ferguson, Korematsu v. United States,* and *Roe v. Wade.*[1] (I have discussed *Roe* already, but I will say something here about its connection to *Dred Scott.*) When George W. Bush, debating John Kerry in 2004, was asked what Supreme Court decisions he disapproved of, he gave *Dred Scott* as an example.

Fewer people know what the decision was actually about, or why it should be criticized. Understanding it requires us to start with the facts.

Dred Scott was a slave owned by one Dr. Emerson, a Missouri resident and a surgeon in the United States Army. In the course of his military service, Emerson traveled from Missouri to the military post at Rock Island, Illinois, and also to Fort Snelling, located in what is now Minnesota but was then a territory controlled by the federal government. He took Scott with him, and he stayed in each place for about two years, Rock Island from 1834 to 1836 and Fort Snelling from 1836 to 1838, after which he returned to Missouri.

Illinois prohibited slavery as a matter of state law. The territory in which Fort Snelling was located did as well, following the Missouri Compromise of 1820, which had admitted Missouri to the Union as a slave state but prohibited slavery in federal territories north of Missouri's southern border. Scott sued Emerson in Missouri state court, arguing that the time spent in Illinois and the federal territory had freed him.

The legal question this presented was a somewhat technical one, in a field known as the conflict of laws. As the name suggests, conflict of laws is designed to resolve cases in which states with different laws have claims to regulate a particular issue—in this case, Scott's status as a free man or a slave. The settled approach adopted a compromise that respected the claims of both the states where people lived and those that they entered. It held that a person's status was determined by the law of his residence. If Scott and Emerson merely passed through Illinois and the federal territory, Scott would remain a slave. But if they stayed long enough to become residents, Scott would be free.

On the facts of his case, Scott should have been entitled to freedom. He had spent two years in Illinois and in the territory, long enough to acquire a residence. But in 1852, when the Missouri Supreme Court decided his case, the compromise approach had fallen apart. The Missouri court refused to grant any effect to the laws of Illinois and the federal territory. It held that Scott was still a slave.

Scott then sued in federal court, and the Supreme Court decided his case in 1857. Chief Justice Roger Taney, writing for the Court, began his analysis with another technical point. Federal courts cannot hear just any case. They cannot exercise any jurisdiction beyond what the Constitution sets out in Article III. The jurisdictional basis for Scott's suit was the clause in Article III allowing federal courts to hear suits "between citizens of different States." The defendant in the federal case, Scott's current owner John Sandford, was a citizen of New York. Dred Scott claimed to be a citizen of Missouri, where he resided at the time of the suit.

Taney disagreed. Blacks descended from slaves, he said, could never be state citizens as far as federal laws such as the jurisdictional requirement were concerned. This was so, he reasoned, because the framers and ratifiers of the Constitution would not have thought that such people could become citizens. The Declaration of Independence, Taney pointed out, announces that "all men are created equal." If the writers of the declaration had thought that blacks could be counted among the American people, they would have been hypocrites to trumpet a commitment to equality while maintaining slavery. And rather than suppose that the Founding Fathers could be hypocrites, Taney decided that they must have been racists, in whose minds blacks "had been excluded from civilized Governments and the family of nations, and doomed to slavery."[2]

If federal law did not recognize Dred Scott as a citizen of Missouri, he was not entitled to sue the citizen of another state in federal court on the basis of diversity of citizenship. Taney's first argument was all he needed to decide that Scott was not entitled to relief and dismiss the case. But he went further, returning to the conflict of laws question that the Missouri Supreme Court had decided. So far as Illinois law was concerned, Taney followed the Missouri Court in ruling that it did not make Scott free. But when he came to the federal law governing the territory, he chose a different rationale. The Missouri Compromise, Taney pronounced, was unconstitutional.

Taney's argument here relied on the Due Process Clause of the Fifth Amendment. But it was not an argument that the Due Process Clause protected fundamental rights that the government could not infringe, the kind of argument used to discover a right to abortion in *Roe v. Wade*. It was an argument about what powers the people had given the federal government—about the kinds of things they had not given the federal government power to do. As I discussed in chapter 6, Justice Samuel Chase wrote that laws purporting to do such things were not laws but mere acts, and their enforcement violated the Due Process Clause.

Taney employed the same reasoning. What he thought the people would not give the federal government power to do was to prescribe that slaveholders who entered a territory lost their property rights to their slaves. As he put it, "An act of Congress which deprives a citizen of the United States of his liberty or property, merely because he came himself or brought his property into a particular Territory of the United States . . . could hardly be dignified with the name of due process of law."[3]

Markers of Illegitimacy

What is bad about *Dred Scott?* The answer is, many things, and I will soon begin listing them. But it is also important to see which of the standard criticisms of the decision are wrong. *Dred Scott* did not hold that the Constitution permitted slavery, as Bush said in the debate, at least not in the sense that that was an issue about which anyone disagreed. In 1857, the Constitution plainly permitted slavery, and in fact contained several provisions protecting it—for instance, the Fugitive Slave Clause of Article IV, which required free states to return slaves who had escaped into their territory.

Dred Scott did not hold that there was a constitutional right to slavery, either, which is Levin's claim.[4] That right existed as a matter of state law, and states could take it away. *Dred Scott's* holding on the Missouri Compromise simply announced that property held under state law enjoyed a strong protection against federal interference. That holding did not invent the doctrine of substantive due process, which I have shown can be traced back much further. Nor is the strong protection of property necessarily an evil principle, though I will suggest it doesn't make much sense. What made its application evil in this case was that people were permitted to own slaves as property.

Last, the problem with *Dred Scott* is not that Chief Justice Taney asserted the power to disregard the original understanding of the Constitution in favor of the needs of his times. *Dred Scott* is a deeply originalist decision. It is a bad example of originalism, in the sense that Taney was probably wrong about the original understanding. But the methodology he employed was a model of originalism, right down to the protestation that while he or others might feel differently now, fidelity to the Constitution requires him to follow the framers' understanding. As he put it, "No one, we presume, supposes that any change in public opinion or feeling, in relation to this unfortunate race, in the civilized nations of Europe or in this country, should induce the court to give to the words of the Constitution a more liberal construction in their favor than they were intended to bear when the instrument was framed and adopted." Unless the Constitution is amended, Taney wrote, "it speaks not only in the same words, but with the same meaning and intent with which it spoke when it came from the hands of its framers, and was voted on and adopted by the people of the United States."[5]

So those are three flaws that do not exist. But if we examine *Dred Scott* to help us figure out what makes a decision bad, we can find others that do. The first is that it is wrong on constitutional meaning, in both of its holdings. With respect to the first holding, Taney ignores the fact that free blacks were citizens of several states at the time of the framing. Given that some free blacks actually participated in the ratification of the Constitution, the idea that descendants of slaves must be categorically barred from citizenship makes little sense. Nor is it necessarily right to characterize suing in federal court under diversity jurisdiction as a privilege of federal citizenship. Article III also gives federal courts jurisdiction over suits between state citizens and foreigners. And if Taney was correct, his ruling meant that citizens of southern states could not sue free black residents of northern states in federal court but would have to rely on the possibly biased northern state courts. Since diversity jurisdiction exists to provide an unbiased forum, that is a surprising result.

As to the second holding, the idea that the people would never give the federal government power to deprive citizens of property merely because they have entered a federal territory is also peculiar. States had that power; it was not doubted that the slaves of owners who allowed them to become residents of free states thereby acquired freedom. And it is hard to see why the people would not give the federal government the power, for instance, to ban alcohol in the territories.

This aspect of *Dred Scott* gives us some basis for evaluating other cases. Decisions that are wrong on constitutional meaning should of course be criticized. But some questions of meaning are hard, and decisions are not illegitimate on that ground unless their error goes so far as to be unreasonable. Taney's conclusion that the word "citizen" necessarily excludes blacks is probably wrong to that extent, though only two justices dissented. His conclusion that Congress cannot prohibit citizens from bringing into federal territories property they hold by the laws of their own state is also probably unreasonable, though Taney's due process reasoning makes somewhat more sense if the question is whether slaveholding states would have given Congress the power to prohibit the ownership of slaves specifically. But where people draw the line between unreasonableness and mere error, I have said, is affected by their own ideological preferences, and we should hesitate to rely too heavily on this criterion. (It is, moreover, simply one component of the approach I have proposed, which first requires a plausible account of constitutional meaning and then asks whether a doctrinal rule is a sensible way of implementing that meaning.)

Another problem with *Dred Scott* is that the decision reaches out to decide a constitutional issue that was not necessary to the decision. In the terms I used in chapter 3, it is procedurally activist. Procedural activism is probably a bad thing, and decisions that engage in it should be criticized. But procedural activism is found in only a small number of cases, and of those, not all are widely considered illegitimate. One of them is *Marbury v. Madison*, in which Chief Justice John Marshall, like Taney in *Dred Scott*, found that the Court lacked jurisdiction over the case but nonetheless addressed the merits.[6] *Marbury* is generally considered not illegitimate but rather foundational, as the first Supreme Court decision to affirm the power of federal courts to hold federal laws unconstitutional. Whether it deserves its lofty reputation is a separate question, but a test for illegitimacy that condemns *Marbury* does not fit well with popular opinion.

Procedural activism suggests that the judge is trying to achieve something more than the resolution of the dispute before him. Taney undoubtedly was; he hoped that the *Dred Scott* decision would bring an end to conflict over slavery. It did not; if anything, it increased national polarization by making moderate Northerners fear that slavery could not be contained to the South but would spread across the country if not eradicated. Another lesson from *Dred Scott* is that ambitious attempts to settle national debates by judicial fiat often backfire.

This is a lesson judges would do well to heed, but it is not a test for illegitimacy. The Constitution does settle some debates, like the one over segregation. Which issues it takes out of the realm of democratic politics is a hard question, and people differ over whether the Constitution has anything to say about, for instance, gay rights or abortion. But we cannot say that any decision that intervenes in a clash of values is illegitimate.

Last, *Dred Scott* intervened in the debate over slavery by choosing the wrong side. The Reconstruction amendments utterly repudiated the decision, abolishing slavery and creating new definitions of national and state citizenships. Choosing the losing side is a reliable and fairly objective test for illegitimacy. Any decision that endorses values the American people later reject will be deemed illegitimate. Unfortunately, winners can be identified only in hindsight. And so that test, too, will not allow us to identify illegitimate decisions as they are rendered. Ultimately, then, *Dred Scott* does not tell us much about what makes a truly bad decision.

Denying Social Meaning: *Plessy v. Ferguson*

In the years immediately following the Civil War, federal troops in the South protected black political participation, which produced racially integrated Republican state governments. But by 1876, Democratic opposition, by means including intimidation and violence, had toppled all but three of the Republican governments. In 1876, the presidential election produced a dramatic deadlock between the Republican Rutherford B. Hayes and the Democrat Samuel Tilden. This election was not settled in the courts; instead Congress appointed a commission to resolve the dispute. The commission voted along party lines to award the presidency to Hayes. Democrats vowed not to accept Hayes, and ultimately agreed only as part of a deal whereby the troops would be withdrawn. With their withdrawal, the remaining Republican governments collapsed.

Under the newly ascendant Democratic governments, racial discrimination returned. The Republican government of New Orleans had integrated its police force and some schools, but in 1890, the Louisiana General Assembly passed a law requiring blacks and whites to sit in separate railroad cars. Homer Plessy challenged the law as a violation of the Equal Protection Clause.

The Supreme Court upheld the law in the 1896 decision of *Plessy v. Ferguson*.[7] *Plessy* is generally considered almost as bad as *Dred Scott*. As with *Dred Scott*, there are indeed reasons to condemn it. But again, it is important to understand which criticisms of *Plessy* are well founded and which are not.

Mark Levin claims that in *Plessy*, an "activist Supreme Court" insisted on "its own segregationist version of what was just" in contravention of the "plain language of the Fourteenth Amendment."[8] This is not really accurate. The Supreme Court did not insist on anything; it simply allowed the state to segregate railroad cars. And it did not reject the plain language of the Equal Protection Clause. That clause does not say that racial discrimination is forbidden, and its framers probably did not think that it would abolish segregation in most contexts, because they likely thought that racial segregation was at least sometimes a reasonable and even-handed approach. If it were, the Equal Protection Clause would not forbid it, any more than it forbids sex-segregated bathrooms.

Where the *Plessy* Court erred was in refusing to accept facts about social meaning that were evident to any reasonable observer. The Court did not deny that some forms of differential treatment would be unconstitutional. Seventeen years earlier, in *Strauder v. West Virginia,* it had struck down a state law prohibiting blacks from serving on juries.[9] In that case, it asserted that the Equal Protection Clause shielded blacks "from unfriendly legislation against them distinctively as colored" and gave them an "exemption from legal discriminations, implying inferiority in civil society." The exclusion of blacks from jury service was unconstitutional, the Court said, because it was "practically a brand upon them, affixed by the law, an assertion of their inferiority."[10]

So differential treatment designed to suggest inferiority would be unconstitutional. As the Court put it in *Plessy,* states could not enact laws "for the annoyance or oppression of a particular class."[11] The key question in *Plessy* was whether Louisiana had segregated its railroad cars for that purpose. The Court dismissed this suggestion cavalierly, observing that the "underlying fallacy" of *Plessy*'s argument was "the assumption that the enforced separation of the two races stamps the colored race with a badge of inferiority." "If this be so," the Court continued, "it is not by reason of anything found in the act, but solely because the colored race chooses to put that construction upon it."[12]

Given the circumstances of Louisiana in the 1890s, however, that was simply not true. This is evident to us now, and it was evident then. Dissenting in *Plessy,* Justice John Marshall Harlan pointed out that "all will admit" that the "real meaning" of the Louisiana law was that "colored citizens are so inferior and degraded that they cannot be allowed to sit in public coaches occupied by white citizens."[13] In a turn of phrase that would become famous, he argued that the "constitution is color-blind, and neither knows nor tolerates classes among citizens."[14]

Plessy goes wrong, then, by refusing to see the plainly unfriendly motive and meaning of the law. Decisions that embrace a clearly incorrect view of the facts are likely to be illegitimate, and this characteristic can be a useful marker. But few decisions do so as transparently as *Plessy*. Moreover, my model picks out *Plessy* just as well. In modern terms, we would say that the Court's mistake was that it deferred too greatly to the supposed legitimate purpose for the law (the avoidance of racial conflict) and ignored the obviously unconstitutional one (the creation of a racial caste system). That is illegitimate, according to my approach, because the white government of Louisiana in the 1890s was highly likely to discount the interests of blacks. The Court should therefore not have deferred; instead, it should have been suspicious that an impermissible motive was at work.

Protecting the Public Interest:
Lochner v. New York

Dred Scott and *Plessy* are well known, even among non-lawyers. *Lochner v. New York* is not.[15] To lawyers and law professors, though, it has long held totemic significance: it represents the imposition of judges' policy preferences in the guise of constitutional interpretation. *Lochner*, most law students are taught, is pure activism.

This view of *Lochner* is no longer held as widely as it once was; one finds many more defenders of the decision than there used to be. I agree with the revisionist account of *Lochner*, and I will try to explain why I view the decision as a good faith mistake rather than a deliberate one. First, though, we need to understand the facts.

As the nineteenth century turned into the twentieth, the American economy was undergoing drastic changes. Jobs shifted into manufacturing, and manufacture was concentrated in factories. Machines reduced the demand for labor and the need for specialized skills, making workers increasingly interchangeable. In these conditions, progressives came to believe that concentrations of private wealth could threaten liberty, and that government could protect it. They enacted laws designed to protect workers from unsafe working conditions and imbalances of bargaining power. The Supreme Court, and state courts, struck down some of these laws, though not all, or even most of them. *Lochner* is one of the most famous of such decisions.

In 1897, the New York legislature passed a law limiting the number of hours bakers could work to ten a day and sixty a week. Joseph Lochner violated this law by hiring a baker to work more than sixty hours in one week. The *Lochner* decision struck down the law, holding that it exceeded the limits of state power and that its enforcement therefore deprived both Lochner and his employee of liberty (the freedom to make contracts) without due process of law.

Critics of *Lochner,* both when it was decided and later, portrayed it as the Court's imposition of its preference for laissez-faire economics on the nation. The Court, these critics charge, believed that the state should not interfere with the free market, and therefore it invented a constitutional right to freedom of contract. Modern critics point out that the Court discovered this right in the Due Process Clause, just as *Roe v. Wade* would later find a right to abortion. *Lochner* and *Roe* are therefore alike, they argue, and *Lochner*'s illegitimacy means that *Roe* is also illegitimate.

This account is mistaken in its description of *Lochner* and consequently also in its attempt to draw a connection to *Roe*. *Roe* and the modern cases are indeed concerned with identifying fundamental rights, a project I have criticized. But *Lochner* did not assert a fundamental right to freedom of contract that the state could infringe only for specially important reasons. The same Court allowed restrictions on freedom of contract in order to protect the health of workers, or the public morals, or for any other legitimate government purpose. The *Lochner* Court was attempting to find the limits of state power, beyond which it could not infringe on any liberty at all.

Why did the Court think that the bakeshop act exceeded state power? Its methodology is the same used by Chief Justice Taney in *Dred Scott* and by Justice Chase in *Calder v. Bull.* It used general principles to decide which goals the state might seek to achieve, and which it might not. One of these principles was that legislation must promote the public good, not the good of particular groups. People created government to promote the general welfare, and they would not have given it the power to play favorites. Thus, the Court struck down laws that seemed designed only to protect workers from imbalances in bargaining power. Whether a law fit that description was a question courts could decide as well as legislatures, and the *Lochner* Court therefore did not defer.

The key question in evaluating *Lochner* is whether the anti-favoritism principle is a plausible understanding of the requirement that legislation serve the public good. The answer is that at one point it might have been. The danger of deploying government power to promote narrow interests was certainly of concern to the framers. James Madison's Federalist Paper 10 is devoted to the argument that the Constitution would be effective in controlling "the violence of faction," whereby "the public good is disregarded in the conflicts of rival parties." Federalist 10 does not seem to think that laws designed to favor particular groups are legitimate exercises of legislative authority, and in a world of self-sufficient individuals it might be hard to see why governmental favoritism would ever be desirable.

But the *Lochner* Court did not inhabit that world. Instead, the world of the early twentieth century was one in which individuals were not self-sufficient, and workers might find themselves, as a practical matter, at the mercy of their employers. It was a world in which governmental regulation might be necessary to avert clashes between labor and capital and to allow the economy to function at all, a lesson brought home by severe strife and economic depressions toward the end of the nineteenth century. In those circumstances, the idea that people would never want the government to redistribute bargaining power made much less sense. And once the question becomes whether redistribution of bargaining power serves the public good, the superior competence of legislatures becomes evident, suggesting the modern deferential approach.

Lochner's mistake, then, was its failure to understand that changing facts might make its conception of the public interest excessively narrow. Governmental intervention on behalf of discrete groups might serve the public good in some circumstances, even if it had not in others. The Court supposed that the question of whether a particular law was in the public interest must receive the same answer at all times, regardless of how society might change. In the terms I used in chapter 3, the Court followed application originalism, not realizing that unchanging constitutional principles can direct different results in different circumstances.

Application originalism is a misguided approach to constitutional interpretation. Justices who employ it should be challenged, the more so if they assert that it is the only legitimate method of interpretation. Like the Court's failure to distinguish between doctrine and meaning, it is a conceptual mistake that can lead to illegitimate decisions. But it will not always do so. Thus, while judges should certainly be aware of its shortcomings, it is not an invariable indicator of illegitimacy.

And *Lochner* itself, I would say, is not illegitimate. The Court clung to a particular conception of constitutional meaning longer than it should have, after facts had proved that conception false. But the meaning was plausible, at least initially, and understanding the constitutional significance of the industrialization and integration of the economy required a massive change in legal thought.

Revolutions in jurisprudence do not occur overnight. In fact, the *Lochner* era persisted until 1937, when the Court backed down in the face of significant pressure from the president and Congress, including Franklin Roosevelt's announced plan to add justices to the Court.[16] The Court-packing plan was defeated in Congress, in no small part because the Court had changed its mind and begun to defer to legislative assessments of the public good. But that change of mind was also likely influenced by the proposal of the plan.

Does this suggest that measures such as the Court-packing plan are appropriate or necessary responses to judicial intransigence? It suggests that they may be effective, though some historians argue that the Court's rethinking of its *Lochner*-era cases was under way before the announcement of the plan and would have proceeded without it. But the intimidation of the Court by the other branches of government may have other, less desirable consequences. It may weaken the Court as an institution, and a weakened Court may defer too much to the other branches. The next case illustrates that danger.

Trusting the Executive: *Korematsu v. United States*

In *Korematsu v. United States,* the Supreme Court declined to interfere with the federal government's World War II internment of West Coast Japanese Americans.[17] *Korematsu* is widely considered a mistaken decision. Most people think that the Court showed excessive passivity, failing to stand up against racial bias. Mark Levin, characteristically, argues instead that an "activist Court" refused to apply "the clear meaning of the Constitution."[18] But both the decision and its failings are a good deal more complicated than either evaluation suggests.

THE DECISION AND ITS BACKGROUND

On February 19, 1941, following the Japanese attack on Pearl Harbor and a congressional declaration of war, President Franklin Delano Roosevelt issued Executive Order 9066. The Order authorized military commanders to designate certain regions as "Military Areas" from which "any or all persons may be excluded." The secretary of war designated Lieutenant General John DeWitt Military Commander of the Western Defense Command. On March 2, 1942, General DeWitt issued a proclamation reciting that the entire Pacific Coast was particularly subject to attack, invasion, and espionage. The proclamation designated as military areas regions including all of the Pacific Coast states and Arizona. Another presidential Executive Order, issued March 18, 1942, created the War Relocation Authority, charged with the creation of a program for the removal, relocation, and supervision of persons excluded from military areas.

On March 21, 1942, Congress ratified the exclusion program with an act making it a misdemeanor to enter, remain in, or leave a military area contrary to the restrictions imposed by the secretary of war or any military commander. Three days later, General DeWitt issued a proclamation imposing an 8 p.m. to 6 a.m. curfew on all enemy aliens and Japanese Americans within the military areas. Beginning the same day, a series of Civilian Exclusion Orders began the process of removing Japanese Americans from coastal regions and concentrating them in camps. Over 120,000 people, mostly birthright citizens, were ultimately confined, spending an average of three years in the camps.

Korematsu is the decision that is most familiar, but it was only one of a series of three cases in which the Court considered the exclusion and detention program. The first, *Hirabayashi v. United States,* dealt only with the curfew orders, despite the fact that Gordon Hirabayashi sought to challenge the exclusion order as well.[19] The decision to limit the *Hirabayashi* decision to the curfew may have been designed to allow the Court more time to consider the exclusion orders, or perhaps to preserve unanimity in *Hirabayashi* itself. (In *Justice Delayed,* Peter Irons reports that Justice Frank Murphy, who had originally intended to dissent in *Hirabayashi,* was won over by Justice Felix Frankfurter's argument that any dissent would support the enemy.)

On June 21, 1943, the Court unanimously affirmed the validity of the curfew order, though three justices wrote separate concurrences expressing some reservations. The Court's opinion acknowledged that "[d]istinctions between citizens solely because of their ancestry are by their very nature odious to a free people." But the principle that "racial discriminations are in most circumstances irrelevant and therefore prohibited" did not bar the government from drawing lines on the basis of race when such distinctions were in fact relevant.[20] The circumstance of a war with Japan, the Court ruled, afforded "a rational basis" for the curfew order.[21]

The decision in Fred Korematsu's case came in late 1944. At that point, the outcome of the war was no longer in doubt, and the continued detention of Japanese Americans seemed increasingly unnecessary. As in *Hirabayashi*, the Court limited the issues before it. Korematsu argued that the military orders required him to report to an Assembly Center, where he would be confined, and that the exclusion order could not be upheld without considering the legality of the detention. Justice Hugo Black, writing for the majority, restricted his analysis to the exclusion order and explicitly noted that he was assessing it "as of the time it was made."[22] After observing that "all legal restriction which curtail the civil rights of a single racial group are immediately suspect,"[23] Black argued that Korematsu had not been subject to the exclusion order "because of hostility to him or his race" but rather "because we are at war with the Japanese Empire."[24]

As it had in *Hirabayashi*, the *Korematsu* Court found a legitimate basis for wholesale exclusion in the military judgment that it "was impossible to bring about an immediate segregation of the disloyal from the loyal."[25] Given this impossibility, Black held that the government had grounds to believe that the exclusion orders were necessary and refused to invoke "the calm perspective of hindsight"[26] to say that they were unjustified. In contrast to *Hirabayashi*, the *Korematsu* Court could not maintain unanimity. Three justices dissented, and one, Frank Murphy, asserted explicitly that the exclusion orders had exceeded constitutional power and fallen "into the ugly abyss of racism."[27]

In the third case, *Ex Parte Endo*, the Court addressed the legality of the detentions, but it avoided the constitutional issue.[28] Instead it focused on the authorization for the detentions, finding that neither the Executive Orders, nor the act of Congress ratifying them, granted the War Relocation Authority power to detain loyal citizens. The government conceded Endo's loyalty, and the Court found her therefore entitled to unconditional release. No justice dissented in *Endo*, but Justice Owen Roberts and Justice Murphy, who had dissented in *Korematsu*, wrote separately to reiterate their claims that the detentions were unconstitutional.

WHAT WENT WRONG?

The internment of loyal Americans on racial grounds was a national disgrace. But it was not the fault of the Court alone. Blame must start with the Executive, with President Roosevelt, who authorized the detentions, and with General DeWitt, who implemented them. It must extend to Congress, which ratified the detention program. The Court confronted a situation in which both of the other two branches of government had expressed a judgment that detention was a necessary war measure. That judgment rested on the assertion of military authorities that substantial evidence, including intercepted shore-to-ship radio transmissions, established that disloyal members of the Japanese-American community were actively aiding the Japanese military.

To reject the judgment of military authorities would have required great self-confidence on the part of the Court. Indeed, viewed from the perspective I have suggested, *Korematsu* is probably legitimate. The internment program affected a racial minority whose interests were not well protected by the political process, and that factor suggested that the Court should not defer. But the basis for the internment program was a military assertion that internment was necessary to stop active disloyalty, and that predetention individualized hearings to separate the loyal from the disloyal were infeasible. That judgment rested on military expertise that the Court did not possess, and that factor suggested that deference was appropriate. With factors pointing in both directions, deference was not illegitimate.

Issuing an order halting the internment program would have been much to ask of any Court, but perhaps especially the Court of 1944. That Court had only seven years earlier been threatened with Roosevelt's Court-packing plan and backed down in a confrontation with the elected branches. The memory of that experience made it extremely unlikely that the Court would render a decision that might precipitate another interbranch conflict and interfere with the war effort.

For all that, the Court was clearly uneasy with the internment program. Its careful limitation of the issues in each of the cases suggests that it was trying to chart a middle course between interfering with a military operation and approving a race-based detention program. It never held that detention was constitutionally sound, and indeed in *Endo* it ordered the release of detainees who could not be proved disloyal. The *Endo* decision was handed down the same day as *Korematsu,* and the justices probably hoped that it was *Endo*'s protection of liberty that would be remembered.

These facts do not excuse the Court's performance, but they suggest the difficulty of its situation, and they demonstrate the justices' unwillingness to accede completely. If this were all we knew, we might conclude that the Court did the best it could, but its best was not good enough. And, as most people do, we would assign ultimate responsibility for the decision to the Court that issued it. But other facts, not apparent at the time, suggest that the outcome in *Korematsu* could have been avoided had the Executive simply displayed honesty and good faith in its dealings with the Court.

Researching a book on the internment cases, Peter Irons discovered considerable discord among the Justice Department lawyers assigned to the litigation. In internal memos, some lawyers had protested that the Department was engaged in the "suppression of evidence" and that General DeWitt's Final Report on the evacuation, presented to the Supreme Court, contained "lies" and "intentional falsehoods." Based on this evidence, Fred Korematsu returned to court in 1983, seeking to have his conviction vacated because of governmental misconduct amounting to a fraud on the Court. Korematsu's petition presented two main allegations.[29]

First, the Justice Department had argued to the courts that there was insufficient time to distinguish between loyal and disloyal Japanese Americans and that a wholesale evacuation was therefore necessary. Irons and Aiko Herzig-Yoshinaga, a research associate for the federal commission created to review the internment program, discovered that DeWitt's initial version of the Final Report had made no mention of insufficient time but asserted that there was simply no way to tell the loyal from the disloyal, a more frankly racist claim to which courts might have been less willing to defer. War Department officials revised the report to make it consistent with the Justice Department's litigating position, burned the original version, and destroyed records of its existence.

Second, the War Department and the Justice Department withheld from the courts and Korematsu's attorneys reports from the FBI, the Federal Communications Commissions (FCC), and the Office of Naval Intelligence that contradicted the DeWitt Report's assertions about disloyalty and espionage activity among the Japanese-American population. Given these contradictory reports, Justice Department attorney John Burling concluded that the DeWitt Report's statements about illegal radio transmissions and shore-to-ship signaling were "intentional falsehoods." Burling drafted a footnote for the Justice Department's brief in *Korematsu* stating that the De-Witt Report's factual assertions in support of the claims of military necessity were "in conflict with information in possession of the Department of Justice" and renouncing any reliance on those facts. At the insistence of the War Department, and over the objections of Burling and his superior Edward Ennis, Assistant Attorney General Herbert Wechsler revised the footnote to eliminate any mention of the contradictory reports. As submitted to the Supreme Court, the footnote simply asserted that the Justice Department relied on the DeWitt report only for facts asserted in the brief.

The government did not oppose Korematsu's request that his conviction be vacated, but it urged the Court not to delve into the issue of governmental misconduct. In its decision, however, the Court explicitly discussed the footnote and its revision, concluding that the government knowingly withheld information from the courts. It granted Korematsu's petition on April 19, 1984.

What this evidence suggests is that blame for the decision in *Korematsu* may lie primarily with the Executive. The real problem in *Korematsu* was not that the Supreme Court was "activist" (a characterization that is, frankly, absurd), nor even that it capitulated to wartime hysteria and racial prejudice. It was that Executive lawyers misled the Court about the basis for the military judgment to which they deferred.

What can we learn from these decisions? If we are seeking foolproof markers of illegitimacy, the answer is, not much.

The four cases cover the bases of judicial review. *Lochner* strikes down a state law, and *Plessy* upholds one. *Dred Scott* strikes down a federal law, and *Korematsu* upholds one. In *Dred Scott* and *Lochner* the Court was too aggressive; in *Plessy* and *Korematsu* it was too passive. And *Lochner* and *Korematsu*, regrettable though they were, were not even obviously illegitimate. What this shows, in the end, is that objective indicators of illegitimacy do not exist. There is no substitute for careful examination of constitutional meaning and the doctrine created to implement it.

But *Plessy* and *Korematsu* have one more thing to teach us. If the Court erred by deferring too much to state officials in *Plessy,* if it was misled by federal officials in *Korematsu,* that suggests that we should be concerned about the performance of these other governmental actors. We cannot decide whether the Court is wielding too much power without considering what the alternatives would look like. That consideration is the goal of the next chapter.

Further Reading

Useful studies of *Dred Scott* include Don E. Fehrbacher, *The Dred Scott Case: Its Significance in American Law and Politics* (Oxford University Press, 2001), and Paul Finkelman, Dred Scott v. Sandford: *A Brief History with Documents* (Palgrave Macmillan, 1997). Mark Graber, in *Dred Scott and the Problem of Constitutional Evil* (Cambridge University Press 2006), suggests that Taney's reasoning was plausible according to the accepted methods of constitutional interpretation in 1857. The evil in *Dred Scott,* in other words, may have come from the Constitution as much as the Court.

Plessy is discussed in Keith Weldon Medley, *We as Freemen: Plessy v. Ferguson* (Pelican, 2003); Michael J. Klarman, *From Jim Crow to Civil Rights: The Supreme Court and the Struggle for Equality* (Oxford University Press, 2004); and Brook Thomas, Plessy v. Ferguson: *A Brief History with Documents* (Bedford Books, 1996).

Cass Sunstein's *The Partial Constitution* (Harvard University Press, 1993) offers one of the earliest revisionist accounts of *Lochner*. Others may be found in Barry Cushman, *Rethinking the New Deal Court: The Structure of a Constitutional Revolution* (Oxford University Press, 1998); Howard Gillman, *The Constitution Besieged: The Rise and Demise of* Lochner *Era Police Powers Jurisprudence* (Duke University Press, 1993); and G. Edward White, *The Constitution and the New Deal* (Harvard University Press, 2000). A detailed study of the facts of *Lochner* is in Paul Kens, Lochner v. New York: *Economic Regulation on Trial* (University Press of Kansas, 1998).

Most of the commentary on *Korematsu* is critical. Notable examples include Peter Irons, ed., *Justice Delayed: The Record of the Japanese American Internment Cases* (Wesleyan University Press, 1989); Peter Irons, *Justice at War* (Oxford University Press, 1983); Greg Robinson, *By Order of the President: FDR and the Internment of Japanese Americans* (Harvard University Press, 2001); and Michi Weglyn, *Years of Infamy: The Untold Story of America's Concentration Camps* (University of Washington Press, 1996). The federal government's report may be found in The Commission on Wartime Relocation, *Personal Justice Denied* (U.S. Government Printing Office, 1992). Taking the other side is Michelle Malkin, *In Defense of Internment: The Case for 'Racial Profiling' in World War II and the War on Terror* (Regnery, 2004).

V
Striking the Balance

13

Branches Behaving Badly: Whom Do You Trust?

M ark Levin's *Men in Black* is a catalog of bad Supreme Court decisions. It establishes that the Supreme Court does not always do the right thing, though I have argued that many of the decisions Levin condemns are legitimate, and some obviously so. The reminder is useful, however, for it counteracts the tendency to portray the Supreme Court as an unfailing engine of progress. Court worship is on the wane, however, and the danger nowadays is more excessive vilification.

Neither of these is correct, for the simple reason that the Court cannot be evaluated in isolation. The ultimate question must be comparative: how does the Court stack up against the other branches of the federal government? Who should be trusted to observe and enforce the Constitution?

History reveals that the Court has not been infallible. Before the Civil War, it was an aggressive protector of slavery; afterward its acceptance of the transformation wrought by the Fourteenth Amendment was grudging and slow. In the early years of the twentieth century, it was a determined opponent of legitimate governmental regulation of the economy. Recently, it has erred by supposing that the doctrine it creates is equivalent to the meaning of the Constitution itself, a conceptual mistake that could also be seen as an illegitimate power grab.

But one would not have to look far, of course, to find similar misdeeds on the part the other branches of the federal government. In 1798, Congress passed the Sedition Act, which criminalized criticism of the government. In 1850, it passed a Fugitive Slave Act that denied accused fugitives the right to testify in their own defense and paid federal commissioners ten dollars for every individual determined to be a fugitive slave, compared to five dollars for every one set free.

Two presidents, Andrew Johnson and Bill Clinton, have been impeached, which suggests misbehavior either on their part (if the impeachments were justified) or on the part of Congress (if they were not). President Franklin Roosevelt authorized, and Congress ratified, the race-based detention of loyal citizens. Executive lawyers misled the Court in *Korematsu*. Scandals involving the Executive are routine, from Teapot Dome in the Harding administration, to Watergate and Iran-Contra. While some of these scandals raise only the specter of corruption or incompetence, others suggest knowing attempts to undermine or circumvent the Constitution.

Each branch of government has done bad things in the past, and each will do them in the future. Each has made claims to power that the other branches have rejected. No branch of government is the good guy all the time; none always wears the white hat. The answer to the question of which should be trusted to guard the meaning of the Constitution is that none should be.

The great innovation of the framers was to create a government that is not our master but our servant. The Constitution gives each branch distinctive powers to avoid dangerous concentrations of authority, and in order to protect the status of the People as the ultimate sovereign. Likewise, each branch has distinctive abilities in deciding whether particular kinds of acts are consistent with the Constitution. Courts are generally good at interpreting laws and deciding narrow factual questions. Legislatures are generally good at balancing costs and benefits and deciding broad or complex factual questions. Executive officials are generally good at tailoring the enforcement of laws to meet the demands of fact and circumstance in individual cases.

These abilities deserve respect as far as they go, and no farther. Authority for determining compliance with the Constitution is properly diffused among the branches in order to preserve the ultimate authority of the American people. The government may exercise interpretive authority as our representative, but its claims rest on that representative function and must ultimately be ratified by popular approval.

From this perspective, there is indeed something troubling about the Court's recent claims that it is the sole body allowed to interpret the Constitution, that its doctrine is equivalent to constitutional meaning. That claim is the root of the decisions I have called illegitimate. It is something the Court should not be doing, and it is encouraging that the most recent decisions have taken a more moderate stance.

But again, the key question is comparative. Under Chief Justice William Rehnquist, the Supreme Court was aggressive in asserting its interpretive supremacy. But the other branches have not been shy in wielding their own powers. Congress has claimed the power to regulate virtually any activity, invoking the Commerce Clause without giving much evident thought to the question of whether the regulated activity does affect interstate commerce, much less whether it is something that might be handled better by the states individually. While I tend to think that these claims did not exceed Congress's power, they may well have abused it.

As for the Executive, it has recently asserted the authority to label anyone, including American citizens, enemy combatants and detain them as long as it wishes with no judicial oversight. With respect to aliens, it has claimed that the Constitution imposes no limits on what it can do so long as it does not bring them within the borders of the United States. It can, if it wishes, torture or arbitrarily execute with impunity. Even Congress cannot prevent this, Executive officials have argued, because the Constitution frees the president from all restraint when he exercises his power as commander-in-chief of the armed forces. Likewise, the Executive has claimed the ability to engage in warrantless surveillance of Americans despite a federal law explicitly forbidding the practice.

Which of these branches is the greatest threat to liberty and the ultimate authority of the people? In Federalist 78, Alexander Hamilton wrote that the judiciary, possessing neither force nor will, but only judgment, would always be the branch "least dangerous to the political rights of the Constitution." That formulation is often invoked ironically these days, as critics argue that the Court has abandoned judgment and embraced will. But I hope this book has suggested that very few of the Court's decisions are truly the product of will.

Even if the Supreme Court does behave willfully, Hamilton's point remains. The Court can render judgments, but it cannot enforce them. Its decisions are effective only so long as people follow them. In the face of sustained popular opposition, the Supreme Court is relatively powerless to impose its will.

In fact, many of the decisions that modern critics complain about are those in which the Court has declined to strike down the acts of a state or another branch of the federal government. Critics believe that the Court has given Congress too much power under the Commerce Clause, erred in permitting any form of affirmative action or campaign finance reform, and failed to enforce the Takings Clause in the recent *Kelo* decision. These are all instances in which the Court has deferred to representative bodies. If so many of the complaints about the Court's performance are that it has been too lax in supervising other governmental actors, the problem is clearly not that judges are abusing their power. And attempts to intimidate the Court will only lead to more such decisions.

In the cases in which the Court has intervened in conflicts between values, such as gay rights or the juvenile death penalty, attacks on the Court might have the desired effect in the short term. The Court can, as Hamilton put it, be "overpowered, awed, or influenced by its co-ordinate branches." But the effect would be brief. In those decisions, I have argued, the justices are not imposing their own values; they are reflecting their sense of an emerging national consensus. Preventing the Court from speaking for a national majority will not stop the evolution of public opinion, and it will not stop that majority from eventually having its way. It is distressing, of course, to see one's values lose their hold on society. But the Court is not the problem, and attacking it is not the solution.

That leaves a far shorter list of supposed judicial power grabs. The Court's decisions about abortion and the Establishment Clause are possible candidates. They do, undeniably, limit the authority of the states. The decisions are legitimate, I have said, but different approaches may be preferable. In both areas, the Court has been moving toward greater acceptance of state regulation, something that I think would also be legitimate. The appointments of John Roberts and Samuel Alito are likely to reinforce the trend. This case law does not represent any sort of constitutional crisis.

More significant in terms of the appropriate balance of power are the recent decisions dealing with alleged enemy combatants. These cases are clear instances of the Court asserting itself against the Executive. But the powers the Executive has claimed here are truly breathtaking. It is not partisan to say this; Justice Antonin Scalia, who is no one's idea of a liberal activist, rejected the Executive's position in *Hamdi* more forcefully than the main opinion. *Hamdi* and *Rasul* are relatively modest pushes back against very aggressive claims of Executive authority. They invite congressional participation, which has been sadly lacking. And they seem to have worked; Congress has recently enacted legislation to define the rights of detainees and specify the scope of judicial review. Involving all three branches of government is the surest way to avoid oppression by any one.

Conclusion

People call the Court activist because they disagree with its decisions. But the kind of people who use the word "activist" are generally disagreeing on political grounds; the decisions they see as illegitimate are the ones whose results they do not like. If constitutional law was nothing more than politics, these criticisms might make sense, though they would also be unpersuasive to anyone who did not share the critic's political beliefs. But constitutional decision-making involves more than politics, and we can use nonpolitical standards to judge the Court.

We can ask, in particular, whether the Court has made a sensible decision about whether or not to defer to the judgment of other governmental actors. This is frequently the most important aspect of a decision, for it frequently determines the outcome of a case. It is, moreover, probably the most important consideration if we are trying to decide whether the Court has assumed more power than it rightfully possesses, for refusals to defer are the form such a power grab would take. I have offered some factors that make deference more or less appropriate in particular kinds of circumstances, and I have used those factors to evaluate the Court's performance. Generally speaking, this perspective suggests that the Court is doing a pretty good job.

There are, of course, some decisions with which I disagree. In those decisions, the Court has adopted a less deferential stance than I believe is warranted, and it has equated its own doctrine with the Constitution. Humility is a virtue in judges, as Chief Justice Roberts noted during his confirmation hearings, and we may hope that the Roberts Court will show a little more than its predecessor.

But humility is a virtue in citizens as well. "The spirit of liberty," said the great judge Learned Hand, "is the spirit which is not too sure that it is right; the spirit of liberty is the spirit which seeks to understand the minds of other men and women."[1] Blunderbuss charges of activism are contrary to this spirit. They are a display of thoughtless partisanship, a refusal to consider the possibility that the "plain meaning" of the Constitution does not embody one's every political desire.

There is plenty of room for argument about Supreme Court decisions. In most of the cases I discuss, the Court's decision is legitimate, but a decision going the other way would be legitimate as well. The Supreme Court typically hears only the hardest of cases, presenting questions about which lower federal judges have disagreed. In such cases, one approach may be wiser or better than the other, but neither is an abandonment of the judicial role. I do not expect that readers will agree with all of my assessments, and that is as it should be. Our job as citizens is to debate these issues, calmly, thoughtfully, and with the presumption that those we disagree with are acting in good faith. I hope that this book will facilitate such debates, by offering a framework within which they can be productive.

I hope, too, that the book will serve as an antidote to the loose talk of judicial activism. That is poisonous stuff, complacent and self-serving in its invocations of a plain meaning that does not exist, alarming in its self-assurance, and corrosive in its refusal to admit the possibility of legitimate disagreement. There have been true constitutional crises in the past, and our system has weathered them without resort to the drastic remedies proposed by current critics of the Court. There is no crisis now, and it would be a serious mistake to let partisan alarmists convince us that any such measures are necessary. Constitutional democracy demands more than the conviction of narrow minds.

Notes

Introduction

1. http://www.fed-soc.org/Publications/hottopics/august.htm.
2. http://www.whitehouse.gov/news/releases/2005/07/20050719–7.html.
3. http://www.whitehouse.gov/news/releases/2005/10/20051031.html.

Chapter One:
The Plain Meaning of the Constitution

1. Dana Milbank, "And the Verdict on Justice Kennedy Is: Guilty," *Washington Post,* April 9, 2005.
2. Derek Rose, "Robertson: Judges Worse Than Al-Qaeda," *New York Daily News,* May 2, 2005, available at http://www.nydailynews.com/front/story/305721p-261517c.html.
3. http://www.defenselink.mil/news/Mar2005/d20050318nds1.pdf.
4. *Planned Parenthood v. Casey,* 505 U.S. 833, 1000 (1992) (Scalia, J., dissenting).
5. Mark Levin, *Men in Black: How the Supreme Court Is Destroying America* (Regnery Publishing, 2005).
6. Ibid., 10.
7. Ibid., 13.
8. First Inaugural Address, March 4, 1861.
9. "A Confession of Faith," August 6, 1912, available in Theodore Roosevelt, *Social Justice and Popular Rule: Essays, Addresses, and Public Statements Relating to the Progressive Movement (1910–1916)* (Arno Press, 1974).

10. Fireside Chat on Reorganization of the Judiciary, March 9, 1937, available at http://www.hpol.org/fdr/chat/.

11. Levin, *Men in Black*, 16.

12. Southern Manifesto, 102 Cong. Rec. 4515–16 (1956).

13. Thomas M. Keck, *The Most Activist Supreme Court in History: The Road to Modern Judicial Conservatism* (University of Chicago Press, 2004); Herman Schwartz, ed., *The Rehnquist Court: Judicial Activism on the Right* (Hill and Wang, 2002).

14. Levin, *Men in Black*, 59.

15. Ibid., 91.

16. Ibid., 143–44.

17. Ibid., 111.

18. *Lochner v. New York*, 198 U.S. 45, 76 (1905) (Holmes, J., dissenting).

Chapter Two:
The Model

1. *Brown v. Allen*, 344 U.S. 443, 540 (1953) (Jackson, J., concurring).

Chapter Three:
From Activism to Legitimacy

1. Franklin D. Roosevelt, "Address on Constitution Day, Washington, D.C., Sept. 17, 1937," in *The Public Papers and Addresses of Franklin D. Roosevelt 359*, ed. Samuel I. Rosenman (Macmillan, 1941), vol. 6.

2. Congressional Record 3–22–72, page S4578.

3. Roy P. Basler, ed., "Fourth Debate with Stephen A. Douglas at Charleston, Illinois," in *The Collected Works of Abraham Lincoln* (Rutgers University Press, 1953), 3:145–46.

4. *Bradwell v. Illinois*, 83 U.S. 130, 141–42 (1873) (Bradley, J., concurring).

5. See *Loving v. Virginia*, 388 U.S. 1, 3 (1967).

Chapter Four:
Equal Protection, Criminal Procedure, Executive Detention

1. *Brown v. Board of Education*, 347 U.S. 483 (1954).

2. Ibid., 492.

3. Ibid., 494.

4. Ibid., 495.

5. "All God's Chillun," *New York Times,* May 18, 1954.

6. See William H. Freivogel, "*Brown v. Board of Education,*" *St. Louis Post-Dispatch,* January 13, 2004 (reporting prior editorial), available at http://www.stltoday.com/stltoday/news/special/pd125.nsf/0/0059A8B0796B FC9586256E04006157A0.

7. Herbert Wechsler, *Principles, Politics and Fundamental Law* (Harvard University Press, 1961), 47 .

8. Southern Manifesto, 102 Cong. Rec. 4515–16 (1956).

9. Richard Kluger, *Simple Justice* (Vintage 2004), 713.

10. Michael Klarman, *From Jim Crow to Civil Rights* (Oxford University Press, 2004).

11. The most notable recent example is perhaps Paul Craig Roberts and Lawrence M. Stratton, *The New Color Line* (Regnery, 1997).

12. The most heroic effort, and the one on which most originalists rely, is Michael McConnell, *Originalism and the Desegregation Decisions,* 81 Va. L. Rev. 947 (1995).

13. *Strauder v. West Virginia,* 100 U.S. 303 (1880).

14. Kluger, *Simple Justice,* 699.

15. Charles Black, *The Lawfulness of the Segregation Decisions,* 69 Yale L. J. 421, 424 (1960).

16. Kluger, *Simple Justice,* 699.

17. *Loving v. Virginia,* 388 U.S. 1, 9 (1967).

18. Ibid. at 7.

19. Ibid.

20. Ibid. at 8.

21. Ibid. at 12.

22. *Miranda v. Arizona,* 384 U.S. 436 (1966).

23. *Dickerson v. United States,* 530 U.S. 428 (2000).

24. See *Smith v. Robbins,* 528 U.S. 259 (2000).

25. See *Hamdi v. Rumsfeld,* 542 U.S. 507 (2004).

26. See *Rasul v. Bush,* 542 U.S. 466 (2004), note 15 (stating that the detainees' allegations "unquestionably describe 'custody in violation of the Constitution or laws or treaties of the United States'").

27. See *In re Guantanamo Detainee Cases,* 355 F. Supp. 2d 443, 454 (D.D.C., 2005) ("Respondents argue that the [*Rasul*] decision was silent on the issue of whether the detainees actually *possess* any underlying substantive rights, and they further contend that earlier Supreme Court precedent and the law of this Circuit make clear that the detainees do not hold any such substantive rights.").

28. See Section 1005(e)(2)(c)(ii), PL 109-148, 2005 HR 286328 (preserving ability of courts to consider constitutionality of detention). While the Detainee Treatment Act provides for judicial review of the conclusions of Combatant Status Review Tribunals if the Executive chooses to conduct such proceedings, it does not entitle detainees to review by a tribunal, and in fact it seems to foreclose judicial relief for detainees who have not been given such review. In effect, then, it seems to authorize indefinite detention with no status review at all, a troubling result. For discussion of the jurisdiction-stripping provision, see Judith Resnik, "Court Stripping: Unconscionable and Unconstitutional?" available at http://www.slate.com/id/2135240/fr/rss/.

29. See *Hamdi*, 542 U.S. 507 (2004) (Scalia, J., dissenting).

30. Mark Levin, *Men in Black: How the Supreme Court Is Destroying America* (Regnery Publishing, 2005), 118.

31. Ibid., 117.

32. Ibid., 122.

33. See *Gherebi v. Bush*, 374 F. 3d 727, 738 (9th Cir. 2004) ("under the government's theory, it is free to imprison Gherebi indefinitely along with hundreds of other citizens of foreign countries, friendly nations among them, and to do with Gherebi and these detainees as it will, when it pleases, without any compliance with any rule of law of any kind, without permitting him to consult counsel, and without acknowledging any judicial forum in which its actions may be challenged. Indeed, at oral argument, the government advised us that its position would be the same even if the claims were that it was engaging in acts of torture or that it was summarily executing the detainees.").

34. *In re Guantanamo Detainee Cases*, 355 F. Supp. 2d 443, 475 (D.D.C., 2005).

35. *Korematsu v. United States*, 323 U.S. 214 (1944).

Chapter Five:
Gay Rights

1. *Bowers v. Hardwick*, 478 U.S. 186, 193 (1986).

2. *Romer v. Evans*, 517 U.S. 620 (1996).

3. *Lawrence v. Texas*, 539 U.S. 558 (2003).

4. *Goodridge v. Department of Public Health*, 798 N. E. 2d 941 (Mass. 2003).

5. Transcript of oral argument in *Romer v. Evans*, 1995 WL 605822, *17.

6. *Romer*, 517 U.S. at 632.

7. Ibid. at 634.

8. Mark Levin, *Men In Black: How the Supreme Court Is Destroying America* (Regnery Publishing, 2005), 75.

9. *Romer,* 517 U.S. at 644 (Scalia, J., dissenting).

10. Ibid. at 636 (Scalia, J., dissenting).

11. Ibid. at 652 (Scalia, J., dissenting).

12. *Ratchford v. Gay Lib,* 434 U.S. 1080 (1978).

13. The following data are drawn from the American Enterprise Institute's "Study in Public Opinion: Attitudes About Homosexuality and Gay Marriage" (2005).

14. *Bradwell v. Illinois,* 83 U.S. 130 (1873).

15. *Plessy v. Ferguson,* 163 U.S. 537 (1896).

16. Transcript of oral argument in *Lawrence v. Texas,* 2003 WL 1702534, *43.

17. *Lawrence,* 569 U.S. at 602 (Scalia, J., dissenting).

18. This list comes from Justice Scalia's dissent in *Lawrence.* Other critics have offered similar predictions.

19. *Lawrence,* 539 U.S. at 579.

20. Ibid. at 604 (Scalia, J., dissenting).

21. *Goodridge v. Department of Public Health,* 798 N. E. 2d 941 (Mass. 2003).

22. Ibid. at 961.

23. Ibid. at 965.

24. Ibid. at 958.

25. *Lawrence,* 539 U.S. at 567.

26. Ibid. at 585 (O'Connor, J., concurring).

27. David A. Fahrenthold, "Massachusetts Lawmakers Defeat Bid to Halt Gay Marriage," *Washington Post,* September 15, 2005, available at http://www.sfgate.com/cgi-bin/article.cgi?file=/c/a/2005/09/15/MNG2NENN841.DTL.

28. *New State Ice Co. v. Liebman,* 285 U.S. 262 (1932) (Brandeis, J., dissenting).

29. "President Calls for a Constitutional Amendment Protecting Marriage," http://www.whitehouse.gov/news/releases/2004/02/20040224–2.html.

Chapter Six:
Abortion

1. *Roe v. Wade,* 410 U.S. 113 (1973).

2. *Planned Parenthood v. Casey,* 505 US 833 (1992).

3. *Griswold v. Connecticut,* 381 U.S. 479 (1965).

4. Ibid. at 485.

5. *Eisenstadt v. Baird,* 405 U.S. 438, 453 (1972).

6. *Roe,* 410 U.S. at 153.

7. Ibid. at 165.

8. Ibid. at 173.

9. John Hart Ely, *The Wages of Crying Wolf: A Commentary on* Roe v. Wade, 82 Yale L. J. 921 (1973).

10. *Roe,* 410 U.S. at 165.

11. *Casey,* 505 U.S. at 851.

12. Ibid. at 866.

13. Ibid. at 846.

14. John Hart Ely, *Democracy and Distrust* (Harvard University Press, 1980), 18.

15. *Calder v. Bull,* 3 U.S. 386, 388 (1798).

16. Ibid.

17. See *Geduldig v. Aiello,* 417 U.S. 484 (1974).

18. *Stenberg v. Carhart,* 530 U.S. 914 (2000).

Chapter Seven:
Takings

1. http://lgraham.senate.gov/index.cfm?mode=speechpage&id=245816.

2. James Kent, *Commentaries on American Law,* ed. O. W. Holmes, 12th ed. (Boston, 1873), 2:340.

3. *Berman v. Parker,* 348 U.S. 26, 32 (1954).

4. *Kelo v. City of New London,* 125 S.Ct. 2655, 2669 (2005) (Kennedy, J., concurring).

5. Ibid. at 2677 (O'Connor, J., dissenting).

6. Ibid. at 2686–87 (Thomas, J., dissenting).

7. Ibid. at 2670 (Kennedy, J., concurring).

Chapter Eight:
The Establishment Clause

1. Mark Levin, *Men in Black: How the Supreme Court Is Destroying America* (Regnery Publishing, 2005), 36.

2. Ibid., 46.

3. 1 Annals of Congress 730 (August 15, 1789).

4. *Slaughterhouse Cases*, 83 U.S. 36 (1873).

5. See Noah Feldman, *Divided by God* (Farrar, Straus and Giroux, 2005), 27–32.

6. *Zelman v. Simmons-Harris*, 536 U.S. 639 (2002).

7. *Wallace v. Jaffree*, 472 U.S. 38 (1985).

8. *Capitol Square Review and Advisory Bd. v. Pinette*, 515 U.S. 753 (1995).

9. *Rosenberger v. Rectors and Visitors of the University of Virginia*, 515 U.S. 819 (1995).

10. *Widmar v. Vincent*, 454 U.S. 263 (1981).

11. *Elk Grove Unified School District v. Newdow*, 542 U.S. 1 (2004).

Chapter Nine:
The Death Penalty

1. *Atkins v. Virginia*, 536 U.S. 304 (2002).

2. *Roper v. Simmons*, 125 S.Ct. 1183 (2005).

3. *Juvenile Logic*, March 21, 2005.

4. *Harmelin v. Michigan*, 501 U.S. 957 (1991).

5. Ibid. at 976.

6. Ibid. at 971 (quoting 1 Journals of the House of Lords 367 [May 31, 1689]).

7. *Weems v. United States*, 217 U.S. 349 (1910).

8. *Harmelin*, 501 U.S. at 994.

9. *Atkins*, 536 U.S. at 315.

10. *Juvenile Logic*, supra.

11. *Atkins*, 536 U.S. at 316 n21.

12. *Roper*, 125 S.Ct. at 1192.

13. Ibid. at 1200.

Chapter Ten:
The First Amendment

1. *McConnell v. Federal Election Commission*, 540 U.S. 93 (2003).

2. Mark Levin, *Men in Black: How the Supreme Court Is Destroying America* (Regnery Publishing, 2005), 143.

3. Ibid., 157.

Chapter Eleven:
Refusing to Defer

1. See, e.g., *Schechter Poultry Corp. v. United States,* 295 U.S. 495 (1935) (holding that wage and hour regulations for butchers do not deal with transactions in interstate commerce).

2. *National Labor Relations Board v. Jones & Laughlin Steel Corporation,* 301 U.S. 1, 37 (1937) (emphasis added).

3. See *Wickard v. Filburn,* 317 U.S. 111, 125 (1942).

4. *United States v. Lopez,* 514 U.S. 549 (1995).

5. *United States v. Morrison,* 529 U.S. 598 (2000).

6. Ibid. at 633 (Souter, J., dissenting).

7. *City of Boerne v. Flores,* 521 U.S. 507, 520 (1997).

8. *Katzenbach v. Morgan,* 384 U.S. 641, 656 (1966).

9. *Board of Trustees of the University of Alabama v. Garrett,* 531 U.S. 356 (2001).

10. *Kimel v. Florida Board of Regents,* 528 U.S. 62 (2000).

11. Ibid. at 83, 87.

12. Ibid. at 64, 88.

13. *Garrett,* 531 U.S. at 367; see also ibid. at 370 ("'adverse, disparate treatment' often does not amount to a constitutional violation where rational-basis scrutiny applies").

14. See ibid. at 372 (noting that the ADA "makes it the employer's duty to prove that it would suffer such a burden, instead of requiring [as the Constitution does] that the complaining party negate reasonable bases for the employer's decision").

15. *Regents of the University of California v. Bakke,* 438 U.S. 265 (1978).

16. Ibid. at 275.

17. Ibid. at 313.

18. *Gratz v. Bollinger,* 539 U.S. 244 (2003).

19. *Grutter v. Bollinger,* 539 U.S. 306 (2003).

20. Mark Levin, *Men in Black: How the Supreme Court Is Destroying America* (Regnery Publishing, 2005), 91.

21. *Grutter,* 539 U.S. at 368 (Thomas, J., dissenting)

22. Levin, *Men in Black,* 91.

23. *Slaughterhouse,* 83 U.S. at 71.

24. Levin, *Men in Black,* 89.

25. See Jed Rubenfeld, *Affirmative Action,* 107 Yale L. J. 427 (1997).

26. *Bakke,* 438 U.S. at 290.

27. *Romer,* 517 U.S. at 633, 632.

28. Laurence H. Tribe, "eroG v. hsuB: Through the Looking Glass," in *Bush v. Gore*, ed. Bruce Ackerman (Yale University Press, 2002), 50.

29. *Bush v. Gore*, 531 U.S. 98, 109 (2000).

30. Tribe, "eroG v. hsuB," 50.

31. *Whitney v. California*, 274 U.S. 357, 376 (1927) (Brandeis, J., concurring).

Chapter Twelve:
Reviled Decisions

1. Mark Levin, *Men in Black: How the Supreme Court Is Destroying America* (Regnery Publishing, 2005), 14.

2. *Dred Scott v. Sandford*, 60 U.S. 393, 410 (1857).

3. Ibid. at 450.

4. Levin, *Men in Black*, 15.

5. *Dred Scott*, 60 U.S. at 426.

6. *Marbury v. Madison*, 5 U.S. 137 (1803).

7. *Plessy v. Ferguson*, 163 U.S. 537 (1896).

8. Levin, *Men in Black*, 16.

9. *Strauder v. West Virginia*, 100 U.S. 303 (1879).

10. Ibid. at 308.

11. *Plessy*, 163 U.S. at 550.

12. Ibid. at 551.

13. Ibid. at 560 (Harlan, J., dissenting).

14. Ibid. at 559 (Harlan, J., dissenting). The claim that the "constitution is color-blind" is now frequently invoked against affirmative action, in support of the claim that no racial distinctions are permitted. But Harlan is quite clear about the kinds of distinctions that violate equal protection: those that create "classes among citizens." (The sentence immediately preceding that one is even clearer: "There is no caste here.") If the implication of inferiority were not crucial, there would have been no reason for either Harlan or the majority to discuss it. So affirmative action is unconstitutional, according to Harlan, only if it marks one race as inferior. I do not think a reasonable observer would conclude that this is its social meaning.

15. *Lochner v. New York*, 198 U.S. 45 (1905).

16. See *West Coast Hotel v. Parrish*, 300 U.S. 379 (1937).

17. *Korematsu v. United States*, 323 U.S. 214 (1944).

18. Levin, *Men in Black*, 17.

19. *Hirabayashi v. United States,* 320 U.S. 81 (1943).

20. Ibid. at 100.

21. Ibid. at 102.

22. *Korematsu,* 323 U.S. at 219.

23. Ibid. at 216.

24. Ibid. at 223.

25. Ibid. at 219.

26. Ibid. at 224.

27. Ibid. at 233 (Murphy, J., dissenting).

28. *Ex Parte Endo,* 323 U.S. 283 (1944).

29. See *Korematsu v. United States,* 584 F.Supp. 1406 (N.D. Cal. 1984).

Chapter Thirteen:
Branches Behaving Badly

1. Learned Hand, "The Spirit of Liberty," in *The Spirit of Liberty: Papers and Addresses of Learned Hand,* ed. Irving Dillard (Alfred A. Knopf, 1952), 189–90.

Index